D1452489

THE HUMANE IMAGINATION

THE HUMANE IMAGINATION

CHARLES L. BLACK, JR.
Sterling Professor Emeritus of Law,
Yale University

OX BOW PRESS
Woodbridge, Connecticut

Published by

Ox Bow Press
P.O. Box 4045
Woodbridge, Connecticut 06525

Library of Congress Cataloging-in-Publication Data

Black, Charles Lund, 1915–
  The humane imagination.
    1. United States—Constitutional law.   2. Law—
Philosophy.   I. Title.
KF4550.A2B52   1986   342.73   86–8797
ISBN 0–918024–43–9   347.302

Printed in the United States of America

For Barbara Aronstein Black,
with love.

CONTENTS

PREFACE

Herein are printed (or reprinted) a few articles, essays and lectures that seem of relatively durable interest. I am most grateful to Harold and Lucille Morowitz for their desiring to bring out this book, and most especially for their very substantial help in bringing their own good judgment to the task of selection.

C.L.B., Jr.

Yale Law School
Spring 1986

THE HUMANE IMAGINATION
IN THE GREAT SOCIETY*

This is my time, after forty-five years, to bring it all back to Texas. I say that I am bringing it back because Texas is where it all came from, and where it still comes from. I have seen many towns, and partly known many minds, since my Texas days, but everything I have done and learned has been built upon the good limestone of Austin.

I shall leave you to imagine what tonight's honor means to me. The Austin schools and the University of Texas gave me my grounding in the *litterae humaniores,* and in those ways of thought into which these more humane letters lead. To name my great teachers from those days would leave time for nothing else. I have never seen or heard of any better school of absolute beginning than the little school in Austin conducted by Mrs. Lollie Orr Huberich, where I started the first grade. I have no cause to believe that any prestigeful Eastern prep school has ever had better teachers, better guides to the humanities and the humane life, than some I remember from Austin High—Nina and Maclovia Hill, Edna von Rosenberg, Florence Ralston Brooke, and many others who were there during the years around 1928 to 1931, when I was there. The University, as we called it, was to me a place of highest intellectual excitement; it was there that I was the one student in a class in Greek composition with Harry Joshua Leon, there that I first read Dante

*The 1983 Texas Lecture on the Humanities, delivered under the auspices of the Texas Committee for the Humanities, to whom thanks are due especially to James Veninga and Roy Mersky.

1

with Carl Swanson, it was there that I sat in a small discussion-group—on medieval history, of all things—headed and guided by Walter Prescott Webb. I could call up very many other great Texas teachers of mine—a cloud of witnesses to the beauty of the learnedly humane life. This talk, on this subject, here in Texas, is a thank-offering in memory of them all.

I chose to do no new reading in preparation for tonight. I am not learned in philosophy. I shall give you my own thoughts as I find and can order them—one person's reflections on his own intellectual, artistic and practical experience.

I did go back and read again, after at least forty years, Shelley's *Defense of Poetry,* looking for the place where he says that ". . .it exceeds all imagination to conceive what would have been the moral condition of the world . . ." if certain poets and other artists had never existed. I discovered, on rereading the whole essay, things that must have gone down into and stayed in my own unconscious, for the thoughts I shall present tonight seem to me very likely to be derived from Shelley's thoughts—not as being identical or even closely similar to his thoughts, but as resulting from the metamorphosis, through long years and in the pressure and heat of my own experience, of some of the themes Shelley started in my mind.

I ought first to say something about the two terms in my title: "the Great Society" and "the humane imagination." I shall not try strictly to "define" either of these terms; as Karl Llewellyn remarked a good long time ago, to "define" is to exclude something, and I feel no urge to exclude anything from either of these concepts, but wish rather, as to each of them, to gesture toward a central zone of meaning, whence and around which may run arcs and circles and lines of influence never to be exhausted.

I have been asked whether I have taken the term, "the Great Society," from the mind and work of Lyndon Johnson. In fact, though I honor Lyndon Johnson for his adoption of this noble term, and for what he did and tried to do in its name, the phrase itself came into my mind a good deal earlier than his Presidency, from my readings in ancient Chinese philosophy, in the selected translations published by E. R. Hughes in 1942, in the Everyman series. I recently opened this little blue-bound book again, after so many years, and almost the first page to which I randomly leafed gave me back the words of Master Meng, Mencius, as the Jesuits taught us to call him:

> Extend the principle of "respect to the aged in my family" to the aged in other men's families, and the principle of "tender care for those of tender years in my family" to those of tender years in other men's families, and the Great Society may be "rolled in the palm of your hand." . . . Thus it is that with the expansion of the scope of your mercy, it is sufficient to protect all within the Four Seas, with the non-extension of its scope it is insufficient to protect your own wife and children. . . .

It may easily have been in that very passage in that little book that I first saw the words "the Great Society." I cannot improve on Master Meng's words, as I believe they can be interpreted and carried into corollaries. I cannot define the Great Society; I do not want to define it, and so to limit its streamings outward, the openness of its arms. But I join Mencius to bow in the direction of the concept as it has entered my own mind from his. The Great Society shows and practices, in its structure and in its workings, respect for *all* the aged, care for *all* the young—and I would add, respect for all the young, care for all the aged, and respect and care for all those who have been young, and who will, in the normal course of nature, one day be old. It is a society whose people strive continually to feel and to value the common humanity that unites them all, and to see in this kinship the defining and holy truth about humankind. It is a society that works into life the illimitable saying of St. Paul: "We are all severally members each of the other."

Let me now make an indispensable point that bridges over into the second of the two terms-in-chief in my title. Care and respect for all are care and respect with regard to feelings and thoughts. Respect is directed at feelings. The reasons for our looking on the failure to maintain and fuel a car as somehow different from the failure to clothe and feed a human being are *feeling* reasons. The Great Society will never rise above its source, which is appreciation for these thoughts and feelings of others.

The Great Society, then, is one which orders itself, and moves within its order, with the goal of taking into account and nourishing the well-being and happiness of all, having continual regard to the feelings and thoughts, the judgments, the desires, of all its members.

It is obvious that we have now bridged over to the other term in my title, "the humane imagination," because the absolutely indispensable means of our dealing with the inner personalities of others is that we *imagine* and continually *reimagine,* as truly as we can, those inner personalities. We "know," as we put it, the inner reality of others, only by imagining that inner reality, and by continually tuning and retuning this imagination, by checking it against clues in language and behavior, by sharpening our own imaginative powers. This is an absolutely crucial point in human relations. To imagine the feelings and desires and thoughts of another person, even with careful attention to checkable clues, is to take a dizzying chance; the continual consciousness that this chance is being taken, every time we think we "know" something about another person's feelings, thoughts or intents, may be one of the principal wellsprings of charity. But to refrain from such imagination is to resign from charity. Imagination is the bridge between human beings, not just once for all, not just now and then, but all the time, all day every day.

Now it is in this kind of imagination—the imagination of the feeling and believing and knowing inwardnesses of others— that I locate the core of what I call the "humane imagination." It is the foundation of all sympathy and empathy. If this humane imagination is lacking, then there can be no respect or care. If this humane imagination is grossly flawed, we deal with grossly mis-imagined persons; efforts, however well intended, are then of only chance effectiveness, and the chances are poor.

I have so far spoken of the *core* of the humane imagination as I conceive it. Whether one thinks of it as a different thing or as a connected part of the same thing, there is another kind of imagination requisite for building the Great Society—the imagination of social and political structures and forms, and of the actions and reactions of persons within these. The attainment of trueness and aptness in this kind of imagination depends altogether on the adequacy and truth of the core of the humane imagination. In a brief introduction, which is all I can present tonight, it will not be confusing to speak of these things together—the humane imagination requisite to understanding people, and the humane imagination requisite for the creation and continual re-creation of forms wherein these people can act and feel.

Very few of us are totally wanting in the humane imagination. With our families, our friends, our colleagues and associates, we exercise this faculty constantly; we are fed many clues; we frequently check the truthfulness of our imaginings. We are strongly and recurrently motivated to make them more true. We may go badly wrong; most of us sometimes do, in small matters or in great. But these wrongnesses may be, in most cases, no more than the inevitable slippages in so chancy a process as that of knowing anybody through imagination. There is always room for improvement, for truer imaginations. But there is comparatively little systematic reason for gaping deficiency in this intimate circle.

"Comparatively?" Compared with what? The answer frames the problem of the humane imagination as the basis of a Great Society comprising innumerable relations which cannot be direct or intimate. Insofar as this problem relates to people circumstanced much like ourselves, the difficulties are still perhaps rather random. But systematic trouble surfaces when we are considering people very unlike ourselves in circumstances and experience.

Let's take a few real problems, turning first to the one around which runs the main tragic theme of our national life—the racism that has poisoned our dealings with black people. That racism, our bitter curse, has many roots and manifestations. One of the chiefest roots and, in turn, manifestations, has been the blank failure of white people to imagine black people anywhere near rightly. A more correct imagination of the inner life of black people, living in an insultingly racist regime, might not at once have brought much change; evil can remain evil, even when it can no longer say with a straight face that it knows not what it does. But it is at least possible that a shift toward humaneness might have started sooner had the humane imagination sooner been put to work on this problem in more minds.

All this applies as well to the failure of male imagination—and often the gross warping into sheer fantasy of what should have been male imagination—with regard to the most inveterate injustice of all, the infamous mistreatment of women, through long, long ages. Here, I think, the main ingredient in the pathology of imagination has been lack of male *will* to try rightly to imagine women, with an extremely large component of a corrupt desire to believe such fantasies about women as would justify the abuses.

A third great defect in imagination, very much with us today, respects our imagination of the chronically poor or even the casually unfortunate. We read of heightened suicide rates, correlated with unemployment numbers, but we imagine only poorly the corrosion of spirit that sets in when, through no fault of one's own, one loses one's job and can find no other work. We poorly imagine the minds of welfare mothers.

Each of these problems in the imagination of others could be the subject of a long lecture. I shall add only one more: The imagination of people of lands and cultures very different from our own. The Great Society must at last be one society comprising the whole human world; only the "normative power of the actual" could make us for one moment think of the present collection of sovereign nations, knowing no common governance, as a satisfactory stopping-place. Nobody could see the near future as a time for realizing the goal of a single Great Society of the world. But the presently insurmountable difficulties need not keep us from walking the first mile, or the first thousand miles, toward a better understanding—a truer imagination—of *all* our kin on earth. For my part, I think I have found, through experience, that the likenesses of the world's people are more impressive than the differences in their characters and traits. Difference is easier to structure and prove. But the likenesses are there, and if we are to be saved it is they that will save us. It is a prime task of the humane imagination to find them, and to make them manifest.

How can this humane imagination be sharpened? The set of answers is as broad as all social experience. The humane imagination commences its work as soon as the cloudy thought begins to stir in the mind of the child that the large moving beings about it have, inwardly, consciousnesses generically like its own. I would not discard the possibility that this first step, indispensable to any further exercise of the humane imagination, is genetically implanted. Parents, friends, teachers must all play their parts, as must the growing person's own longing to understand a world so largely and importantly made up of others. But on this occasion it is appropriate to stress the part that has been played, and may be played, by the *litterae humaniores*, understood in an extended sense—humane letters, the arts of poetry, fiction, and drama, as well as that kind of work in history, anthropology, or other fields, that may be called humanistic, because it works not by describing and counting externalities, but by exercising the humane imagination on the human past, or on alien cultures. Personal experience, remember, is at its most powerful in helping us to imagine persons much like ourselves, while the arts I have named are not so bound, but reach into all the vertical and lateral and horizontal and even temporal distances of the Great Society.

Consider the drama, that art of great age and of infinite profundity and fascination. The drama can be a chief nourisher of the humane imagination. It teaches, by vivid and repeated example, what it means to imagine people altogether other than oneself. The playwright builds an imagination of the persons of the drama, and imagines the interactions of these persons. The director imagines in a more concrete way the working-out of the playwright's imaginings of persons and of happenings. The actor, at the most specific level, imagines another self altogether, and bodies forth that self—magically, in the case of the great artist. Observation of and reflection upon the imaginative work of these people can build profound insights into the work of the humane imagination. But an important lesson emanates too from the imaginative work of the audience. Each spectator is called upon to imagine the inwardness, the feelings and thoughts, of a person known not to exist. There may occur, and doubtless very, very often does occur, a spontaneous acquiescence in illusion; if the imaginations of the playwright, director and actor are well enough accomplished, the spectator loses comprehension of the fictional character of what is being seen and heard. But there must sooner or later return the knowledge of that fictive character, and with it some new appreciation of the immense power of the humane imagination, of the infinitude of its range.

Fiction does not differ by the whole sky from drama. I will concentrate only on the difference at the terminal point, the point of reading. Imagination is called upon to bring forth, out of the reader's self, persons never so much as seen. This process is too complex for extended exploration now; it varies with variances in the fiction-writer's technique—in the use or non-use of assertive explanation, of assumed direct insight into the characters, and so on. But it always calls for strenuous and powerful exercise of the humane imagination by the reader.

I stress the power of these arts to *exercise* the humanc imagination, to *exhibit* its working, rather than their content. The
quality and tendency of the content must vary infinitely. The
quality and tendency may be very good, very bad, or anywhere
in between. The strongest contribution of the dramatic and fictional arts to the Great Society ought not to be a propaganda
but a continual display, in ranging variety, of the powers of that
same humane imagination that must be used to generate the
understanding of one another—the sympathy and the empathy—needful for our building toward the Great Society. At the
same time, I cannot resist mentioning a few examples—mere
examples chosen from thousands of instances—of influences
these arts have had upon the substance of my thinking.

I shall never forget the passage in which Faulkner describes
an old black man in Mississippi as more than resigned to his
own approaching death, because he is ready to have done with
this whole heavy business of being a black. This short passage
contributed to my own understanding of the grinding predic-
ament our black people were in. It shouldn't have. I should have
gotten to just the same place without it. But in fact it did. It
summed things up; it wrote in the elusive last line.

I remember reading, in a little magazine that I cannot now
locate, a story about a family that was waiting in a hotel in
Huntsville until the time came to go get the body of a son and
brother who was to be put to death that night; again, I ought,
without the help of such a story, to have imagined to conclusion
the suffering that the infliction of the penalty of death may impose on altogether innocent people who love the condemned
person, but this story—and how I wish I could find it—summed
it all up, wrote the last line, and enabled me to feel—to imagine—John Spenkelink's mother, waiting in the crowd outside
the prison, as a real mother.

Anthony Powell stresses and abundantly illustrates the overwhelming importance of the *will* in human affairs; this is the
dominant insight in his powerful novels. Having been so instructed by him, I feel I am better able to go to the heart of

many troubles—to see, for example, in our hesitations, in this rich country, about the relief of poverty, not an "economic" difficulty, not any kind of "practical" difficulty, but a radical deficiency of will. I return here to Mencius, Master Meng:

> When the king inquired what the difference in form was between 'not doing' and 'not being able to do,' the reply was, 'With regard to taking the T'ai Mountain under your arm and jumping over the North Sea, if you say to people that you cannot do it, your words represent the truth that you cannot. (On the other hand) with regard to helping an older man break off the branch of a tree, if you say to people that you cannot, this is "I do not," not "I cannot." Thus it is that your failure to exercise royal authority is not in the class of picking up the T'ai Mountain and jumping over the North Sea, but it is in the class of not breaking off a branch.'

We talk about the protection of our fellows from the suffering and indignity of want as though it were a matter of taking Mount Rainier under one's arm and jumping over the Pacific Ocean, when in fact it is a matter of deciding whether or not to help a frail person lift something that we can ourselves lift, even though at some cost.

This in turn has made me desire very much that the poor be better imagined, for I know nothing that would be more likely to break this ice-jam of will than a truer imagination, on the part of powerful people who never were really hungry, of what poverty is like, looked at from within the person afflicted. Humane letters can here often help us along. For one example out of myriads, I remember that Ma Joad, in Steinbeck's *Grapes of Wrath,* had always kept a little souvenir—a dish or a cup, I think—of the St. Louis World's Fair of 1904. When I saw that scene in the film, I remembered that my mother had often spoken with pleasure of her own trip, in her girlhood, to that same Fair. I was pushed along a little further towards seeing the Ma Joads of this world as people, just like those more fortunate materially, but people who have suffered the stupendous misfortune of being crushed by impersonal forces. Edmund Burke, quite rightly, asked the poor to realize of the rich that "they, too, can be broken-hearted." It seems to me that the stern need of our time is an intense realization—an intense imagination—running in just the opposite direction.

I will give one further example, huge and thrilling, of the visible power of humane letters over life—the example of Iceland. Rather few people know very much about Iceland. I have fallen in love with Iceland. Iceland is a vibrant, modern country, with a diplomatic service, a working parliamentary democracy, a good health-care system, bus lines throughout, airlines foreign and domestic, next to no unemployment, efficient postal and telephone service, sophisticated medical research, a small but fine University, excellent schools, effective police, a life-saving service for the mountains, handsome public buildings, two splendid theater companies in Reykjavik, a new national opera of distinction, and so on and on through everything it takes to fill out the picture of a materially and spiritually thriving nation—including an all-suffusing national pride, utterly untainted, as far as I have been able to tell, by any feeling of superiority. The Icelandic economic system is sparked by brilliant ingenuity and powered by hard work.

Iceland prints more books *per capita* than any other country, and a good many generalized and special-subject magazines of high quality. They have motorship service around the island, and motor-vessel service overseas. Still, I'm only sampling. A friend of mine there recently sent me a photocopy of the Crito, part of a published Icelandic translation of Plato's works; he could have sent me translations into Icelandic of *Macbeth* or *Paradise Lost*. I have in New Haven several of Agatha Christie's works, and other detective stories, translated into Icelandic and printed in Iceland; I like to try to read these, because it's a good way to acquire the up-to-date idiom. The several fine Icelandic newspapers, including the world-class *Morgunblathith,* help here, too. Iceland throbs with life.

Now how many people do all this? *Less than 250,000.* Think

about that. That's about as many people as Corpus Christi, about half as many as El Paso. The country is by no means favored with rich natural resources. It has behind it many centuries of oppression, alternating with neglect, by the European country of which it was until this century a dependency. Poverty was long the rule; mass starvation sometimes occurred. As Laxness, the Icelandic Nobel Prize laureate, has pointed out, Iceland, though not really a very cold country, got the name of being cold because for centuries its people had no proper houses or clothing.

Modern Iceland, in short, is a miracle. The cause of the miracle is not mysterious; Laxness has named it, and I know no Icelander who disagrees. The cause is a literature—the ancient poetry, the great sagas—put together in the Middle Ages. That literature has been held in the consciousness of virtually all Icelandic people through all the dark centuries. It has brought it about that Icelanders see themselves as a special people—not superior, but special—the descendants of Vikings and heroes, of heroes in deeds and heroes in endurance. The modern people of Iceland have felt challenged to repeat in their own times and ways the heroism of the past. And they have always seen themselves thus; the great literature was in place, and carried them through grim centuries of endurance, down to the time when national independence and fresh visible achievement became possible. There is no meaning in the speculation whether the self-view kept in life by this literature was "true." The fact that these people held to it, held to the great Icelandic literature, made it true. Indeed, holding on to that literature, and to the implications of that literature, through all those hard ages, was in itself a heroism as great as those told of in the literature itself.

What if the whole world had and cherished a literature that could support in the minds of all its people, through dark times, the vision of a Great Society, to be built despite all difficulties?

But, then, we do have such a literature. I have quoted from it—from the version of Mencius, the version of St. Paul. It is a venerable and widespread literature. If we could come to cherish it, as most of us do not now really cherish it, then our blockage of will might be dissolved, and the humane imagination might at last get to work on building the Great Society.

It would be all but an obscenity to come to the end of a talk on this theme with a sense of having finished.

I have not said what I would like to have had time to say about the value, in the forming of the Great Society, of the rich imaginations in poetry of the kind that resembles myth and dream—the Forgotten Languages of which Erich Fromm reminds us, in a book that was seminal in my young mind. Such poetry is itself a work of the humane imagination; it searches for truths about the human soul that cannot be told in symbols nearer to prose. I have spent a good many of my hours in the solicitation of poetry, some of it of this kind. I am very sure that the mythic and dreamlike, the seemingly unrational but nevertheless strangely moving things in the higher reaches of poetry and of the other arts, are at least as instructive on the human condition and fate as more rationally ordered material can be. Max Beckman's mysterious first triptych, "Departure," says more to me about the heights and deep longings of the human spirit than all but a few paintings more literally interpretable can do. And it is in such sublimities and questings—as we can, perhaps truthfully, imagine them—that the far destinies of the Great Society are hidden. Or so I imagine—I hope with truth.*

*A lecture is to me a thing in itself, and I have not wanted to add anything to (or take anything away from) the text from which this lecture was delivered. But I want to say in this note that the recent happy occasion of the renewal of correspondence with Madame Tamara Toumanova, one of the great ballerinas of this century, has brought it into my mind that, at this point, I should have widened my vision a little more, to include the dance among those wordless arts that have the power to quicken and to enrich, in ways no less mighty for their being mysterious, the humane imagination. The dance is ritual; ritual teaches. I should have remembered that Havelock Ellis's *The Dance of Life* (a title that tells the whole story) was an important book to me when I was very young; I only wish I had taken its teaching more to heart.

Music, too, surrounds and nourishes the humane imagination, giving it sacred tone. In my own case, I do not know whether my hatred of racism and poverty is the more sustained by considerations that can be given words, or by music. Fortunately, the question is one that does not need to be answered; indeed, it needs not to be answered.

I have not been able to say anything about the imagination of justice—an imagination that confronts the humane imagination with the imagination of an order of rightness somehow supporting or standing above the human world. Let us hope that the imagination of such an order of justice is a true imagination, for if it is untrue, our most earnest efforts have no goal. Humane letters constantly invoke and illustrate this imagination of justice; I think of the cinemas, *Twelve Angry Men* and *Oxbow Incident,* but I might have thought of thousands of other illustrations. I must add here that in my view the worst defect in the concept of justice commonly held among us is its not including, as an obligation of justice, the obligation to bring about a fair distribution of material goods; this ought not be seen as a matter of "compassion" but as a matter of right—the human right to that material base of life without which all other human rights are mere mockeries. We need better to imagine the justice of livelihood.

To see any subject clearly and in its fullness, we must travel a little beyond its own bounds. Here I think of another cinema, *Alice's Restaurant,* perhaps over ten years old now. Near its beginning, a disused church building, having been bought by Alice and her husband for use as a restaurant, is ceremonially "secularized" by priests of the Christian denomination to which it has belonged. Meanwhile, a young guitarist and singer makes his way, through great difficulties and even dangers, to meet his friends—the restaurateurs to be and their circle—and to help by making a radio commercial for the new restaurant business. He composes a song, the title song of the film, with the refrain, "You Can Get Anything You Want At Alice's Restaurant." The restaurant opens. The people live their lives around it—human lives of pleasure and sadness. Most of them seem to be trying to do their best, often in a fumbling way. There is love moving among them, but sometimes they are unfair or untrue to one another, and they are sorry. They laugh and they cry. There is good luck and misfortune.

Among them is a young motorcyclist, who is trying to break free of a drug habit. He struggles, but we sense that he is caught in this dreadful fate, doomed. At last, he is killed on his motorcycle, and these people, who loved him, bury him in what used to be a churchyard.

But if you are listening for the deep chords in this story, you see that he is not being buried in what used to be a churchyard. He is being buried in a churchyard. Now we know why the picture was named after the building. The sad striving lives of these people, their laughter and tears, their attempts at kindness, their loves, their frolics, even their quarrels and failures, have reconsecrated the church—or invoked its reconsecration, if that be a different thing. Now the song in the radio commercial yields up its meaning. "You Can Get Anything You Want At Alice's Restaurant": *Ask and it shall be given you; seek and ye shall find.*

Whether or not I have correctly interpreted or even quite correctly recalled this film is not of first importance. What is important is that the humane imagination, playing on the lives of people, may, on reaching its own frontier, encounter there another imagination beyond the humane—the imagination of a holiness that can touch and suffuse human life, that reaches to meet and to consecrate human striving. That imagination is hardly a new one. I am reminded of another saying of Mencius: "Heaven does not speak. The only thing it does is to reveal by deeds and events."

Let us pray that this imagination of holiness be a true imagination. But meanwhile let us use the humane imagination as best we can, toward the well-masoned building of the Great Society—by such light as we have, by such plans as we can draw on our own. That is the only work to which, as work, we can address ourselves. It may be that we will at the same time be performing our part in a long ritual of consecration. I cannot think this would altogether have surprised Erasmus or St. Thomas More, who were of the greatest of the dawn humanists.

In our years, early along, let us, following Mencius, respect one another, care for one another, try, with the help of the humane arts, to imagine one another with growing truthfulness, hopeful that at last the Great Society—to borrow the words that Mencius used of the "great man"—may "dwell in love, the wide house of the world."

LAW AS AN ART*

For many years I have been telling my students that law is an art—just like that. When I had the honor to receive this invitation to present a lecture of a jurisprudential cast, it seemed to me that I could do no better than to ask myself what I had been meaning by this all the while—and then to explore the answers with you here.

As you may well guess, I have found this task less simple than either I or others might thoughtlessly have expected it to be. The utterance of an aphorism is a great deal easier than exploring it into its grounds and implications. I bring you, therefore, not a finished expounding of this short assertion, but rather an account of some of the thoughts it has started in my mind, as I have looked at it from all sides for this occasion.

The first thing I want to say is that, by design rather than by neglect, I have not read anything in preparation for this talk. I am very certain that I am indebted to Karl Llewellyn; anybody who explores any jurisprudential topic today has to be indebted to Karl, and I know that the artistic and aesthetic quality of law was of special concern to him. There are undoubtedly others of whose influence I am not conscious. But I have considered that the best thing I can give you on this single occasion is myself—my own reflections from thirty-two years in law—rather than a cento of quotations, or an answer to an answer to an answer.

Secondly, by way of introduction, I am glad to be able to

*Fourth Annual Distinguished Lecture in Jurisprudence at the University of Tennessee College of Law, delivered 6 April 1978 in Knoxville.

say that the short statement that forms the title to this lecture no longer wholly satisfies me. If the title you have given in advance to a piece of discourse satisfies you after you have done composing it, the indication is strong that you haven't gotten anywhere. There have been times, during my wrestling with this subject in my mind, when I have thought the title needed radical change. I have thought at some junctures, for example, that a better title might turn out to be "Law As A Non-Art"; at other times, reading some recent decisions, I have given some thought to the title "Law As A Mess"—a characterization which we all know could be exhaustively illustrated through a considerable range, and one which, sufficiently generalized, might be thought jurisprudential, if somewhat rudely so.

I have stuck to my original title, though with a ponderous gloss, which I will now put upon it. What I shall end up talking about is the thesis that in some ways, and for some purposes, it is useful and illuminating to look on law as an art. My short title, then, may be taken as stating an assumption which may lead to some interesting insights into some phases of law.

I am not eager to try a definition of law, for I do not expect to succeed where everybody else has failed for about three thousand years. But let me just say that, for my purposes—here and now—there are some approaches to law to which my thesis does not apply, in the sense in which I put that thesis forward. I am referring to the whole set of methods of viewing law which proceed from the outside—the construction of statements, more or less concrete, about the state of the law, or of the legal system, or of any parts thereof. When I say this, I am thinking here of the methods and results of legal history and of legal anthropology, even where our own tribe is the one under study. I think it extremely likely that the methods and approaches of these disciplines that look at law from the outside partake in their own way of artistic quality. Even mathematics and the physical sciences proceed by intuition, by creative leap, to their most significant results, though those results themselves may and must be checked out by rigorous reasoning and test. The same must certainly be true of the work of those who seek sheer insight, for insight's own sake, into any legal culture, past or present.

But I have been concerned with law in a different way—in a way perhaps more natural for most of you, and certainly more natural to me. I have been concerned with law from the inside, with the *practice* of law in the broadest sense, with the use of law to shape the world. And it is predominantly if not entirely from that viewpoint that I shall explore my subject here.

There is wide-reaching contact between these two different ways of approaching law. The facet of contact is broader than might be thought at first sight. It is obvious that the enterprise of using law—the practice of law in its widest meaning—must draw upon sound knowledge of the legal system within which one works. That is only to say that a carpenter must know his materials and tools. But the contact of the purpose-oriented with the anthropologically- or historically-oriented is broader than that. For the practical lawyer—the purpose-oriented lawyer—may draw suggestions of enormous significance from legal cultures of times and places other than our own, and so may hope to change the very methods of the system within which he works. In my own work, for example, I have tried to do my part, along with others, toward domesticating within our own system of constitutional law the method of reasoning by analogy from express constitutional guarantees—a method I am informed is normal in some other legal cultures.

But, despite this broad contact, the aims of the two different approaches to law are very different. The student of law from the outside wants to understand, for the sake of understanding, certain verbal and non-verbal behavior, in its connections with other behavior; this understanding may be sought as to present or past, as to here or there. The practicer of law wants to shape that behavior. I need hardly say that any one person may figure in both these roles. But when I assert that law is an art, or even ask the question whether law is an art, it is this latter sort of activity I have in mind. This is a limitation—but limitation is another name for form, for intelligible contour.

Now, having confessed myself to be one interested in law as a means to ends, as something to be used for something, let me quickly add: I neither occupy nor wish to be thought to advocate a position of crude result-orientation. The avoidance of this cast of mind is especially vital to the constitutionalist—or perhaps I feel that because that happens to be the shop where I work. One may be forced, as I have been forced, to take positions directly adverse to immediate and particular results one favors. I am thinking of my own firm view, frequently reiterated, that a state may validly rescind its consent to a proposed amendment before the requisite three-quarters of the states have assented, even though that question happens to arise in connection with the pending Equal Rights Amendment, which I favor. But this is not an instance of total freedom from result-orientation in a broader sense. The result I want is a constitutional amendment process that is wise and fair and politically sound at all times and for all amendments—one that always requires a genuine contemporaneous consensus by the required number of states.

I am not now soliciting your assent to my view as to rescission, but am putting it forward only as an illustration of the fact that the term "result-oriented" may have many levels of reference. In its usual meaning, it is a pejorative term. But in a broader and much different sense, all good work in law is oriented toward a good result, or more modestly, a result judged good if one includes within the good in law not only soundness of result at an appropriate level of generality, but also visible legitimacy on the intellectual level—an essential, I would think, or hope, to the long-run public acceptance of results.

One more explanation of what I have put forward as the purposive or practical part of the pursuit of law: I am referring here not only to the work of advocates, whether they be advocates in the conventional sense or advocates without clients or commitment to particular cases, but also to the work of judges and even counselors—all who work toward sound results in a legal system.

These successive limitations and expansions of my own scope of reference may be thought, and in a sense perhaps correctly, to make it obvious that law, as I use the term, is an art. I have said that I am concerned with activities directed toward using the materials at hand in a craftsmanlike manner to produce desirable results. It is clear that some people, at least, look on law and practice law in this way. This seems to me to bring law within the range of human enterprises, from painting to medicine, to which we commonly give the name of art.

Perhaps some of the most helpful implications of this view of law-work lie in what it tells us as to what law is not. Above all, law in the sense in which I am using it is not a science. Most lawyers would, I think, readily assent to this verbal negation; we have gotten past all that. But I find that many of those who assent verbally still remain in a state of chronic disappointment at the working out in practice of the fact that law is not a science. When they are driven by experience to the knowledge that results in law are very often not predictable, that the system of law at any one time is invariably an imperfect system, not traceable with entire consistency to widely general principles, they tend to look on these things as defects. From the point of view of the lawyer as artist, these qualities are not defects. To the purposive craftsman in law, the legal system as it stands—or perhaps I should rather say, the legal culture as it stands—is, in its most interesting aspect, the aspect that makes the art of law practiceable, a set of possibilities. These possibilities are more or less likely of occurrence, and the likelihood of their occurrence is influenced by human work. Here the analogy with all the serious arts is, I think, plain.

Let me use as a first example the chain of events that is to me the best illustration in our century of the power of the art of law—the vast development centering around the Brown case.

In retrospect, as to its ultimate merits, the Brown decision seems inevitable, as near a thing to syllogistic reasoning from soundly validated premises as can be found in law. Yet the process by which this decision was attained, and the events following its attainment, were dominated by intuition; its successes and its failures are in great part successes and failures of intuition rather than of logical or scientific judgment.

If the Brown decision was right, then it was right all along. If law were a science, the correctness of the Brown result would have been provable, and the decision could successfully have been demanded, at any time. Instead, we were dealing with intangibles which, in retrospect, make it clear that the Brown decision would have been flatly impossible thirty years earlier; indeed, this was plain at the times involved. The strategy of the attack on the segregation principle has now been exhaustively studied by historians. The interesting thing about it for our present purposes was that that strategy, necessarily, was formed not by principles of a simple cast, as though one had had to do with a mere engineering problem, but rather by a series of informed but only partly rational guesses as to how the Court could be moved, and the country brought to accept that movement. I might add that the progress of professional thought in the Brown case illustrates how slowly the obvious may be accepted—and therefore how important the strategy of procuring this acceptance may be. Jellinek speaks of the "normative power of the actual"—one of the most illuminating of insights into law. I can testify, for I was there, that *Plessy v. Ferguson,* now quite visibly a disingenuous bit of legal shoddy, seemed in 1950 to be quite a serious piece of work, just because it was there— the "normative power of the actual." Bringing about a general recognition of its shoddiness was a work not only of the intellect but of strategic intuition.

The immediately ensuing sequel to the Brown case was a series of *per curiam* decisions outlawing segregation by law in a range of situations outside the school situation which had been under focus in Brown. The range was broad enough that it was plain that the entire regime of segregation by law was finished. There was beyond doubt some intellectual dissonance here. The Brown opinion had centrally emphasized the importance of education, to such an extent as to make it readable as holding nothing outside the school situation. One would have expected the Court to explain its broadening of the antisegregation principle into other fields.

That it did not do so, then and there, was a function, I think, of an intuitive perception, or seeming perception, as to what was politically possible. The pervading evil of all segregation of blacks was intangible—segregation by law was a stigma, a brand, an assertion of inferiority of the race set apart by law. This was true in school and out of school. But this social meaning could be established to the hilt only by a recital placing segregation in its historical and contemporaneous context in the South, for meaning is always established by context. This recital would have been ineffective unless it were entirely candid, and it could not be entirely candid without being highly offensive to the South, where euphemism about race still ruled the day. The Court therefore, it is my guess, chose the easier route, as it then seemed, of placing its results, in Brown perhaps and certainly in the *per curiam* decisions following, on a rationale that did not cover the whole ground.

The point now is not that this tactical decision was either right or wrong. I happen to think it was wrong. To me, a decision not to confront reason squarely is a decision that is just about always wrong. But the point I am making here is that this was a decision based largely on intuition, on unprovables and imponderables, rather than on anything resembling syllogistic reasoning.

The same must be said, of course, of the "all deliberate speed" formula adopted with respect to the implementation of Brown. The doctrinal material here was very simple, and really stated a question rather than a solution. Of course a court of equity is empowered to delay its remedy where circumstances strongly indicate the prudence and fairness of this course. If nothing exactly like the delay allowed in the school segregation cases had ever been allowed before, that fact could hardly be dispositive, for no problem exactly like the school desegregation problem had ever occurred before, and no one could say that, as to this problem of unprecedented magnitude, the court of equity was doctrinally barred from allowing delay. But as I have said, the doctrine, as legal doctrine so often does, merely stated the questions, and provided no answer. The answer of the Court—that expressly sanctioned delay would in the event work out more wisely and more fairly than the formal requirement of immediate compliance—arose not out of legal doctrine but out of the Court's own intuitions as to the developments in the future.

Again, it does not matter, for my purposes now, whether the Court was right about this. My own intuition has always been, and remains, that the Court was wrong—that the South had, in the very nature of the litigation process, more than ample means of delay, and that the open sanctioning of delay, in the "all deliberate speed" formula, needlessly blurred the perception of the people that segregation was flatly unlawful. But what I am interested in now is that *neither* resolution of this question—neither the one espoused by the Court nor the one espoused by many of the rest of us as advocates and writers—could possibly be established by cold reason, or by scientific demonstration, as right.

The crucial tactical judgments, then, in the Brown case, were in great part intuitive. The successes were successes to a great extent based on intuition. The failures, if they were failures, can be pronounced such only as the basis of intuition—which is to say that we really don't know whether they were failures or not. My own profound conviction is that the "all deliberate speed" formula did more harm than good. But such an opinion is insusceptible of demonstration; it can never be decisively proved that the adoption of this formula did not significantly and beneficially work to signal a kind of reasonableness, on the part of the Court, that made the medicine in the end less unpalatable. And who can say, for sure, that this did not, among other things, make barely acceptable the all-important zeal of Lyndon Johnson for civil rights, and the affirmative cloture votes of some border-state Senators on the Civil Rights Act of 1964?

In such a system, one cannot work as a scientist, or as an engineer. One has to deal with intangibles of such numerosity and complexity as to call out the intuitive faculties, whether for persuasion or for decision.

But it would be a great mistake to think that this statement applies only to questions of strategy separate from the merits, or only to great constitutional cases.

It has been very good for me to keep working and teaching in admiralty, because doing this has kept me continually aware of the fact that the intuition factor in law is by no means confined to great constitutional cases, but is to be found everywhere. When I look over the whole range of leading admiralty decisions, I am struck by the fact that virtually none of them was even arguably compelled by prior authority; all were wide open to considerations of justice, fairness, and convenience. Let me just list a few:

The extension of admiralty jurisdiction over non-tidal waters, and over waters within the territorial jurisdiction of states.

The extension of admiralty contract jurisdiction over many contracts, such as the contract of marine insurance, relating to maritime matters, though made and to be performed on land.

The interpretation of the Limitation of Liability Act to cover personal injuries and other torts, and pleasure boats.

The outlawing of negligence clauses in bills of lading, the beginning of a long development that culminated in the Carriage of Goods by Sea Act of 1936.

The enunciation, and 120 years later the abandonment, of the role of even division of damages in both-to-blame collision cases.

The development of a national law, non-statutory in great part, regarding seamen's injuries.

I could go on and on, boring you with a catalog of decisions as long as the Homeric catalog of ships. What I think I could not do is give you any kind of a list of leading cases in admiralty of which it could be said that they rested on that kind of truly compelling reasoning from authority which we regard, when we don't think about it, as normal for law. I cannot now think of a single one.

Now if I am right about this, think what it means—and what it has meant to the view of law held by one who is predominantly a constitutionalist. Those who know only constitutional law might think that the political factors that play upon that law make it, in a word, less "legal" than other law. But maritime law is commercial law, fraternal twin to the *lex mercatoria*. If its principal lines of decision originate in something other than compelling reason—and that is a very conservative statement of the case—then we have defined a system within which one can successfully work only by giving full scope to such intuitive factors as one possesses.

You will have misunderstood me altogether if you take what I have said as a denigration of reason. To me, responsibility to reason, even to technical reason, is the soul of the art of law; of this more later. But when I look over the cases I have described and mentioned, it seems to me that, taken as a whole, they exhibit both the necessity and the desirability of our finding both effectiveness and peace in that kind of reasoning which is actually, and ought to be, most effective in law work—reasoning from facts and from projected effect. The insufficiency of pure authority opens the technical reason of law to just these considerations; possibly the central problem of the art of law is just that of finding and using these openings.

In an old courtroom I knew as a child, on the bench where the judges sat, there was inscribed the Latin phrase meaning, "Let Justice Be Done Though The Heavens Fall." Even as an adolescent, having perhaps, even then, a naturally legal mind, I wondered why the fall of the heavens should be the feared consequence of the doing of justice. It seemed to me the heavens were much more likely to fall if justice were not done.

But I take it that the most probable meaning given to this phrase by those who ordered its inscription was, "Let correct law be applied though great damage ensue." In principle, I would assent to that. But one of the consequences of steadily looking on law as an art is that you find the question rarely comes up. For if you seek, you will usually find that the materials of law are adequate to the task of doing right, as far as we can see the right. Not always, but most of the time. And nothing so energizes the search, within law, for the means of doing justice, as does the conception of law as the art of doing justice.

Justice? Of course nobody can define it; nor, at last, will there be entirely general agreement on its attainment. This, too, tends to mark law as an art, for the very same things may be said of beauty, the goal of the fine arts such as painting and music and poetry, and perhaps even of health, the goal of the art of medicine.

I said I had read nothing in preparation for this lecture, and in a narrow sense that is true. But I did not intend to assert that I had never read anything in my life. And I have read, long ago, the late Edmond Cahn's book, *The Sense of Injustice*. And, as I remember, he very correctly based this book on the insight that *injustice* is a great deal easier to spot than justice is to define. And the unjust result is usually a failure of the art of law—a botched piece of work.

Let me go back and examine in more detail one of the admiralty decisional lines to which I referred a few minutes ago.

If the owner of a pleasure boat sends it out in seaworthy condition under the direction of a seemingly competent crew, and if the master, despite his antecedent seeming competence, gets drunk and runs down several smaller boats, killing two people and maiming three others, then the owner of the boat may limit his liability to the value of the boat, which will often be very much less than the damage done. Indeed, if the boat has in the course of these accidents itself been damaged, and has sunk in such deep water as not to be worth the cost of raising and repair, the owner goes scot-free, and can even keep the property insurance money he gets for the boat.

I wonder if anybody can possibly think that is a just result. Once, in San Francisco, I was talking to the maritime bar there, mostly defendant-minded people, and I asked them, "Would anybody here care to undertake the defense of the justice of the application of Limitation of Liability Statute to pleasure yachts?" No one spoke up. I cannot think anyone could have anything to say to this question.

How did it happen? Well, in 1851, with some amendments later on, Congress passed the Limitation of Liability Act, saying that the owner of any "vessel" might limit his liability to the value of the "vessel." This act, on its face, appears to have in contemplation a commercial context. Its background was a fear, on the part of vessel owners, of liability to the owners of lost or damaged cargo. Yet "any vessel" means "any vessel," and a pleasure-boat is a "vessel." Q.E.D.

Now you and I know that such a conclusion is one that willfully or carelessly ignores the resources of the art of law. Absolute literalness in the construction of a statute, without regard to its background or purpose, is never compelled. The reports are crowded with cases where general statutory language has been cut down to reasonable size by standard canons of construction. The pleasure-boat owner's limitation is at once a monstrous injustice and a very obvious sheer technical failure in the use of law's resources.

If it were an isolated example, it might not be very interesting. But I must say that in my experience such shocking injustices as this have almost always been traceable to some kind of obtuseness with regard to technical possibility. The techniques of our law were sharpened for attaining the sensible, the just result. They are not always adequate to justice, or to the correcting of injustice. There are some musical compositions that you couldn't play on the piano. But I repeat, it is overwhelmingly true that if you seek ye shall find, in the technical weaponry, the means needful for a fair outcome.

I have suggested that this is not always true. This in turn suggests that there is some limit on the malleability of legitimate legal technique. The realist insights of the early decades of this century have made it difficult to give form to this limit. Interestingly enough, a variation on the insight of Edmond Cahn is easily applicable here. While it is hard to define, generally, the limits that the legal system places on the quest for justice, it is comparatively easy to set forth instances wherein these limits would plainly be violated by a given result, however desirable such a result might be. I believe that the present position, as to the limitation of liability of pleasure-boat owners, is such an instance. I have indicated that, in my view, the original extension of this limitation rule to pleasure-boat owners was a gross injustice, and at the same time an inexcusable failure to employ the simplest rudiments of the art of statutory interpretation to the problem. But the position has drastically changed since this failure occurred. In 1936, Congress amended the Limitation of Liability Act so as to augment the amount of the limitation fund applicable to personal injury claims. In the statute accomplishing this, Congress referred unmistakably to the limitation available to the owners of private yachts, exempting them from the new augmentation of liability. After this Act of Congress, I do not think I could, as a judge, possibly conclude that pleasure yachts were not covered; the originally mistaken result has been, as I see it, accepted and confirmed by Congress. The effect, it seems, is to block quite decisively a new judicial look at this problem. This is not, of course, to block a new look at the problem in Congress, but it does make very difficult a new look at the problem in litigation. The injustice remains as great as ever, but, at the level of litigation, and of judicial judgment, a just solution seems incompatible with sound legal method.

The art of law is founded upon and practiced within a set of tensions between aims not simultaneously realizable in full. On the one hand the aim of attaining justice—or, at a lower level, practicability and political, commercial, or human-relations wisdom—and on the other hand the aim of using the authority of law in a legitimate manner, employing but not straining the techniques sanctioned as legitimate within our legal culture. Living and working within this tension is not made the more easy by the fact that no reasoning about justice or even about practicability, and no reasoning about legal legitimacy, can ever be altogether demonstrative, like a demonstration in mathematics or even in physical science. What can be asked of the artist in law is not that he present or espouse utterly certain conclusions—if he tries for this, indeed, he is following an *ignis fatuus,* trying to play a sonata on a sunbeam—but rather that he continually explore, with disciplined imagination, the means to justice within the legal system, and that at the same time he be continually responsive to the demand for reasoned justification within that system. The continued search for creative resolution of this tension is one of the main things the art of law is about.

This tension is not without its counterpart in other arts—the tension between ideal result and limitation of means. Yet every artist of any kind knows that this tension is far more than a mere strife between opposites. Music as we know it is limited by the intervals between tones; most of the sonic spectrum is not used at all. Yet it would seem that music as an art is not only limited but also made possible by this fact; it has yet to be shown—as against a background of thousands of years—that music can be music without severe limitation. In painting—which I practice as an amateur, simply because there is no law against it—the case is hardly less clear. Virtually all painting of any artistic value is limited to a single plane surface—so drastic a constriction of whole reality that it is said that some peoples, not familiar with the convention, cannot recognize painting as representational at all. Anybody who paints even a little is impressed or even astounded by the fewness of really useful pigments. The values of luminosity in paint cannot approach the range of variation found in reality. Yet, again, these limitations not only bind but also free the art. I think I see, dimly and from a great distance, the truth that the quest of law for justice, though limited and occasionally thwarted by the technical necessities of law, is in much greater measure made possible only by these very limitations. I doubt that the idea and the ideal of justice would ever have come into being if the idea and the ideal of constraining and constrained law had not also come into being. And it is certainly true that in music, in painting, and in law, the technical apparatus, fully mastered, engenders suggestions of rightness which might not otherwise have presented themselves to the mind. The late Frank Bozyan of Yale, an artist in music and in life, once told me—in one of those great sayings that stick with you forever—that the aim of all training in singing is that the student at last learn to sing naturally. I profoundly believe that the final result of training in law is that one may come close to thinking naturally about problems of justice. It is visibly true of law that a really high technical proficiency liberates instead of binds—and this is one of the surest diagnostic signs of art.

I would interpose here a thought about the present trend, in some academic circles at least, to discard altogether the traditional techniques of law, and simply to drive toward what is conceived as the right result, usually on the basis of something labelled a "philosophy." I regard this as a potentially baneful tendency—first, because it seems to me certain to erode public acceptance of the legitimacy of legal work, and, even more importantly, because it passes over the almost infinitely rich re-

sources of traditional law—including, always, the tradition of
ordered development and changes—in favor of comparatively
thin and incomplete systems of thought. My mind goes to jazz
music, very possibly the most brilliantly innovative music of our
century. Much has been said about the newness of jazz, and it
was indeed a creation in the full sense. But perhaps too little
has been made of the conservatism of jazz—its general allegiance to the tradition of western music—in tonality, in har-
mony, in time-signatures, in counterpoint. The irrepressible
Louis Armstrong, on an early record, says "watch that chord."
I wonder what kind of music we would have gotten in place of
jazz if nobody had watched that chord, but had started afresh
with an utterly new theory, or meta-theory, or meta-meta-theory
about sound in an ideal society—or, to be utterly fashionable,
a "model" or three competing "models," of the place of sound
in society. I do know that the jazz we got started out and in
large part stayed with the main stream of traditional musical
technique; finding therein some limitations, to be sure, but also,
and how much more significantly, the ground and material for
the brilliantly new. I think law is like that, and must be like that
if it is to retain the precious feel of legitimacy and at the same
time use not mere closet constructions, but all the experience
of all the ages for its working material and means, for its own
brilliant innovations. The conception of law as an art might call
us back to this way of work.

One should not go too far with express parallels between
law and the other arts. Painting is not music, medicine is not
architecture, and law is not any of these others. It does resemble
them generally in that it uses the means at hand toward the
creation of something convenient—comparable, perhaps not
too fancifully, to entertaining dance-music, pleasing decoration,
or, more closely, to a building that will stand up and serve its
purpose—or something beautiful, for justice is beautiful, and
even an approach to justice is an approach to beauty.

Still, I have been struck as I have gone along by some chance parallels between law and the other arts. I was so struck, for example, when I read Sir Joshua Reynolds' remark that the look of reality in painting results from showing a clear line when the line is clear, and not showing a clear line when the line is not clear. When a portrait looks like a cut-out, it is because the artist has not attended to Sir Joshua's maxim. One of the eternal problems, constantly recurrent, in the art of law is the problem of clarity, or certainty. Roscoe Pound somewhere says that the problem of certainty in law is the masterproblem of jurisprudence, around which all others revolve. Some lawyers talk as though they thought maximum clarity always desirable even though they wouldn't have to probe very deeply to find that fraud, and fiduciary obligation, and undue influence, have been carefully isolated from exact definition, because such exact definition would simply point out safe ways of immunity, and, to the birds of prey, make the law "their perch and not their terror."

Or take what is called "state interference with interstate commerce." Anybody who reads these cases can see that no clear line either has been or can be drawn. If you look on law as an intellectual exercise, the aim of which is always maximum clarity of line, you can get quite upset by this. But I wonder whether that is the right way to look at the matter. I think that the function of these cases is rather to signal that somewhere in there, not too far from limiting trucks to ninety inches width, and not too far from making trucks change their mudguards at the state line, there is a limit on what states may do, as against economic nationhood—itself a concept as vague, nearly, as it is necessary to national life. Paradoxically, the drawing of a really clear line could result either in the strangulation of state activity or the hopeless hindering of economic nationhood. Perhaps vagueness is what is needed here, for one of the serious aims of law—aims far more serious than the aim of entire clarity every time. I think illustrations of this kind could be multiplied throughout law.

I have said only a little of what I had hoped to say. Most

regrettably of all to me, I have felt that a decent respect for the attention span of man and womankind forbids my touching on the creativeness of the dealings of law with fact, with making a case, with the subject of evidence considered affirmatively rather than as a set of exclusionary rules. I hope to return soon to this. I console myself with the thought that the very difficulty of saying abstract things about law as an art tends to mark law as being an art in truth. It is, I confess, an art that I feel much more comfortable in practicing than I do in talking about abstractly. Perhaps, after all, the aphorism, with its suggestive power, is the most important thing. I repeat, then, that, to me, law *is* the art of governing the world, the art of producing justice. Sooner or later, in all these lectures, one finds one is calling across the years to the young people in the audience. To them, tonight, I say: I have found this concept of law as an art life-sustaining; it has kept me on my feet in law. Reflect upon it. If you find it even somewhat helpful, you can have it free. If you do not think it helpful, may you be blessed in your own way.

THE TWO CITIES OF LAW*

O n the ground of man's public life, two shapes of law may be discerned—sometimes in mutual complement, sometimes in contrast.

First, there is the law that prevails in society. Courts decide cases and give reasons for their decisions. Statutes are printed and read. Precedents are recorded and used as lawyers' ingenuity may devise. People enjoy legacies, lose cars to the finance company, get married, go to the penitentiary. And as a matter of psychological fact, there exists, in the minds of judges and lawyers, a conceptual framework to guide and explain all this activity. This structure of legal ideas is not exactly the same in any two minds, but there is enough agreement for law to do its work—and even the fact of disagreement is a fact about law as it exists. This law that palpably prevails in each nation may be called "positive law."

Second, as misty as a Chinese painter's mountain, but as insistently there as the Chinese painter makes his mountain seem, is another shape of law—the image of law as men in their time think law ought to be. This ideal law cannot be known, as positive law can be known, from the deeds and words of lawyers and judges at their professional tasks. Those who would persuade us of its requirements cannot point to the readable print of code or reported decision. All we can know from all these

*Reprinted from *The Occasions of Justice* by Charles L. Black, Jr. New York: The Macmillan Company, 1963. Copyright Charles L. Black, Jr. 1960.

sources is the tenor of such law as exists and prevails—and that may be good law or bad law.

Yet we are compelled to seek the shape of right law. By taking up this quest, we may be transgressing the canons of scientific positivism, but if we do not take it up we strip ourselves of the insignia of humanity. And so from the earliest inscriptions in pyramid tombs down to the latest article in the *Yale Law Journal,* from the Cheyenne Indian before Custer to the man riding up-town on the Broadway Express, we try and always have tried not only to know the law as it is but also to discern, however dimly and uncertainly, what it may be that justice requires of law.

This search for light in law has taken many forms. Recurrently through Western history, the name "natural law" has been given to the projected image of law as it ought to be. Aristotle and Cicero wrote of a law of nature, against which human positive law was to be measured. Aquinas brought the concept within his mighty synthesis. Grotius built it into the foundations of modern international law. John Locke made the idea a perdurable part of liberal thought in England, whence it crossed the Atlantic to enter our own Declaration of Independence, in that document's opening appeal to "the Laws of Nature and of Nature's God. . . ." "Natural-law" thought permeates the epochs of our intellectual tradition.

Natural law, as conceived by its proponents, bears none of the marks of positive law. It is not set up by the state; no court shapes it; no legislature establishes or changes it. Instead, its expounders have been philosophers and publicists, professors and ecclesiastics. Each proposition in each natural-law system can claim validity solely on the basis of arguments advanced by people who write books on the subject. Their reasoning starts with stated or assumed beliefs about the nature of man; from these beliefs are drawn conclusions as to what law ought to be. The end product, when fully developed, is a system of *ideal* law, which can be held up as a model for comparison with positive law.

Hugo Grotius, one of the greatest of the natural lawyers, shortly stated the underlying assumption:

> The law of nature is a dictate of right reason which points out that an act according as it is or is not in conformity with the social and rational nature of man has in it a quality of moral baseness or moral necessity, and that, in consequence, such an act is either forbidden or enjoined by the author of nature, God.

In the reach of historic time not one but many systems of natural law have been elaborated in this way. These have differed widely. But the root idea remains surprisingly constant; from it "natural-law" thought takes its name. In age after age it has been maintained or assumed that there is a right law, a just law, inferable by reason from the nature of man, and of his relations to his society and to the cosmic order.

It is implausible—though not impossible—that so richly accredited a tradition should turn out after all to be entirely worthless. It is therefore surprising that what may fairly be called the dominant view in British and American jurisprudence today rejects the concept of "natural law," and waves away the whole corpus of natural-law speculation. It is not that any single system of purportedly "natural law" is rejected, but rather that the value of natural-law reasoning as a whole is denied—expressly or by eloquent disregard.

This attitude can be explained on a number of grounds, not all of them necessarily applicable to the case of any one thinker. Most fundamental is the widespread modern view that only delusion beckons when we conceive of "justice" as having anything remotely like the objective reality which invests the positive institutions of law. We have no warrant, say the followers of this view, for supposing that there exists any "justice" which can be "discovered"; "justice" is merely a name for our own reactions. The difference between good law and bad law, between the just and the unjust, lies in the feelings of men; the goal, conceived as possessing shape and reality of its own, is a mere wishful imagination.

Others, without opening this ultimate issue, object to the term "natural law," with its implication that the goals of law are themselves a kind of law. Nothing but confusion inheres, they say, in this willful blurring of what exists with what is desired. Nor, others would have it, can "natural" law really be inferred from man's "nature." Eskimo infanticide is as "natural" as our school-lunch funds; something beyond a knowledge of natural facts is required for our discriminating between these institutions.

Objection is also made to the lack of sharp, critical analysis in natural-law speculation. "A man," runs a recurrent natural-law precept, "is entitled to the fruits of his labor." "Property is to be protected," says another. Such formulas, to begin with, are largely if not entirely tautological; a man's "property" might well be defined as that which the law will protect or ought to protect for him. Insofar as they are not tautological they cannot be logically deduced from any validated generalizations about known human nature.

Of course, agreement with such vapid *sententiae* is easy to procure, regardless of logical gaps in their derivation. But such agreement means nothing, for the precepts themselves are too vague to solve real legal problems, and often tell with equal force on both sides of the same controversy. Is the recipient of a public old-age pension receiving the "fruits of his labor"? Or is the taxpayer who supports the pension being deprived of his? If you unknowingly buy a ring from a jeweler who unknowingly bought it from a thief, is it in justice your "property" or that of the man from whom it was stolen? The real problems of law involve not faithful obedience to beauteous maxims, but the mediation of competing claims, each with a measure of soundness.

And—the critics go on—even if we could, by speculation

on the nature of man, reach warrantable and clear conclusions as to the goals of law, another formidable hurdle remains. The decision whether a law is good entails judgment not only on the desirability of its goal but also on its practical working. A father who will not be kind to his children, who shrugs off their problems, who willfully refuses to help them past the crises of growth, may be thought worse than a nonkilling bank robber; the correction of his behavior may be a more appealing goal than the suppression of bank robbery. But would putting court injunctions on such men actually improve the relations of fathers with their children? What would be the social results of licensing off-track bookmakers? On the answering of such questions—questions about how a legal device will really work—altogether depends the sane evaluation of each rule and practice in law. They never can be answered more than tentatively; they cannot be answered at all by deduction from grand principles.

The schools of natural law, say the critics, are actually narrow and particularistic. Their splendid reasonings from the nature of man, universal as may be their phrasing, are fancy masks for the prejudices of a single time or sect or current of thought. Their "obvious" truths are obvious to the already convinced; their "deductions" seem compelling to those who have already accepted the conclusions. Truism and fallacy are the warp and woof of their loose, gaudy fabrics.

Each of these objections has great weight. Yet—as Professor Lon Fuller and others have shown—there remains a value in the concept which the term "natural law" seeks to suggest. Let me try to get at this value by talking not in philosophic but in practical terms—in terms of what we actually find ourselves doing when we seriously ponder questions about law.

First, the impulse to shape the institutions of law toward more perfect justice is felt and obeyed by all kinds of men. It is surprisingly uncorrelated with philosophic views as to the objective validity to be imputed to "the good" or to "justice." Some of the people who, as philosophers, assure us that "justice" is merely a name for our own emotions, are tireless in advocacy for justice as they conceive it; their advocacy does not consist merely in exhibiting their emotions but also in giving reasons why other people ought to experience the same emotions. We need not ask here whether they thus contradict themselves; let us note instead the sheer fact that all people, everywhere, are given, when they consider law, to thinking and working and talking for law's betterment.

But before we can seek to improve our law, we must attain some fairly clear conviction as to what goals are to be desired. The considerations and arguments with which we give shape to these goals may take many forms. But surely all sensible thought about the improvement of law must start with something like this assumption: *Good law is law that is good for man in his society and in the world.*

Of course, one cannot deduce any specific consequences from this formula. But the formula has nevertheless a certain clarifying power. For it reminds us that the quest for good law entails not only the forming of conviction about some abstract good but also the acquiring of knowledge about man—about the nature of man—and about the nature of his societies and of his world. Such knowledge alone may not tell us anything about justice, but it is an indispensable part of all thought about justice.

Finally, when we think deeply about shaping law toward justice, it always happens that we begin to think in some degree systematically. Problems of justice in law rarely present a single simple question. Many values are likely to be at stake. A measure of system is the alternative to chaos.

But a more or less systematic view of the requirements of justice, based in large and essential part on a more or less systematic view of the nature of man, begins to look like "natural law." One might almost say that it is the nature of legal man to think along natural-law lines. We do not have to construct all-

inclusive systems of ideal law. We need not attribute to our partial and tentative conclusions the strutting, self-anointed pseudo
infallibility which has flawed much natural-law writing. We need
not assume that knowledge about man's nature is enough; some
value judgment, some act of sheer moral choice, must be added.
But the route we must take, if we are to think to any purpose
about the ends of law, goes in much the same direction as the
path that natural-law thought has followed.

Whether we use the words "natural law" is a question of
terminology. The essential thing is not to discard the good in
natural-law thought, merely because we cannot accept all its past
claims. Much natural-law speculation is pretentious, arrogant,
and absurd. Much of it consists in trivial juggling of high-
sounding expressions. But we could put up with all this, and
with more, rather than reject the idea that human positive law
ought to move toward a goal, however flickeringly and unsurely
perceived, and that this movement cannot dispense with considerations—as soundly validated as may be and as clearly structured as the material honestly allows—about the nature of man,
the maker and subject of law.

It is not surprising, therefore, that natural-law thought has
had extensive and continual relations with the positive law of
the United States. The relationship, to be sure, has been a peculiar and largely a disguised one. An American lawyer could
live out his professional life at the bar and on the bench without
ever hearing the term "natural law." Our lawyers and our judges
talk positive law—their reasonings concern precedents, statutes,
and constitutional provisions. Reference to the justice of the
case, apart from positive law, is likely to be apologetic, and almost never purports to rely on systematic natural-law concepts.
How, then, can it be said that natural-law thought has entered
into the fabric of American legal culture?

To answer this question we must consider the separate

senses in which American law has rejected and accepted natural-law thought. Let us begin with the rejection.

Early in our history the idea was put forward that natural law ought to be treated as a sort of law freely invocable in court and superior to other kinds of law. This would mean that, if the judge believed that a statute or constitutional provision outraged natural justice, his duty would be to disregard the positive law and to decide the case contrary to its command.

This notion was utterly and finally rejected; the judiciary dropped it like a hot potato. That the dogmas of any school of juristic philosophers should control and nullify the positive law of statute and Constitution, put in force by the people through their established organs of legality, was and is gratingly inconsonant with the theories of our political life. The suggestion was an insolent one; it was met with rebuke and slid into oblivion.

The result—and here we reach the acceptance—is that such force as natural-law thought may have in American law must operate not from outside but within and through positive law. So much of it is accepted as the people, through their representatives, are willing to accept—and no more.

Yet the acceptance has been large; judgments about right and justice, formed in part on the basis of beliefs as to the nature of man and society, permeate every level of our legal process. The most obvious illustration is that of formal legislation, including the Constitution and its amendments. The constitutional ban on the ex post facto law—the law punishing actions committed prior to its passage—implemented the belief that such laws contravened natural justice. The abolition of imprisonment for debt was motivated by convictions as to the rights of man. Our social-security laws rest on systematic thought about the nature of man's social relations. But any finite list of examples tends to minimize the connection between legislation and prevailing concepts of justice. Our laws on marriage, wills, taxation, and criminal procedure—these and uncountably more—are determined in significant part by widely held views as to the requirements of justice, in the light of beliefs about man's nature.

It is less obvious, but clearly true, that in the decision of particular cases judges not only may but must fill out the incertitudes of positive law with something like natural-law considerations. This is an all-pervading part of our legal process; the aggregate effect is of major importance in the whole shaping of positive law. We have often thought of the judge as a kind of logic machine, deducing his result from precedents and statutes. Sometimes this is a substantially true picture; when the applicable precedents or statutes speak with a clear voice, the conscientious judge must normally obey, whatever he may think of the justice of the matter. But there are cases in infinite number in which this cannot be what happens—not because the judge is wayward but because the law does not contain a single incontrovertible answer to the problem presented.

Our law is found in great part in precedents, in prior decided cases. But no two cases are ever entirely alike. The judge must often decide whether the difference is *enough* to justify a variation in result. This question cannot be answered by logical reasoning on the basis of precedent; it is a question that arises after such reasoning is completed.

The other major component of our law is statutory—the law of legislative acts. Very often the key terms used in a statute are quite vague; always there are borderlands of uncertain applicability. Sometimes it can be shown that vagueness was intended, that Congress or a state legislature deliberately left it up to the judges to make concrete the statute's generalities. But intended or not, the consequence is that the law does not unambiguously tell the judge what to do.

The judge, therefore, cannot always obey the command of precedent and statute, because the command often cannot be made out with clarity. This is nobody's fault; it is inherent in the nature of thought and language. Who would expect that something called "the law" could settle in advance every question posed by the infinite variety of life? It is both unsurprising and true that our legal system has large leeways, within which the narrowly technical materials do not speak clearly. This is not a defect, but the means by which law remains flexible and capable of growth.

But the judge must decide each case. If honest assessment of the "purely legal" materials does not produce decision, then what is to fill the gap? There are three possibilities; each of them plays a part, and in the particular case they may be complexly related.

First, the judge may try to make out the "principle" of the statute or of the lines of precedent, and then determine how this principle applies to the case. This principle, if discernible at all, must be, broadly speaking, a principle of justice, a judgment as to the requirements of good law. Such a principle cannot be understood without understanding the reasons for it. And these reasons, as we have seen, will commonly follow the lines of natural-law thought, in the generic sense which we have explored.

Secondly, the judge may have recourse to what he thinks to be communal feelings of justice. These, too, are often based on reasons sounding in popular apprehension of natural law; certain it is that ordinary people think and talk in terms of natural law and natural right.

Thirdly, where these more impersonal techniques fail to determine decision, the judge may be brought to his own views of the justice of the matter.

Now these three paths to decision are not really so categorically separable as might appear. Neither the "principle" of statute and case law nor the "sense of justice" of the community is at all easy to determine, and in every case these things actually take effect, in the process of decision, as they are registered in the mind of the judge. The underlying principle is the underlying principle as he discerns it; the communal feeling is the communal feeling as he senses it. But each of these three modes brings into the decisional process somebody's definition of justice and somebody's reasons—often of a "natural-law" kind—for proposing this definition; the judge must be able to handle and weigh such material.

And if he is any good at his job, he will not discharge this necessary part of it on a sporadic basis. He will have thought connectedly on the goals of law and on the good of man—to enable him both to clarify his own thoughts to the point of usability in his work and to understand the thoughts of others, where these must be brought to bear on decision. He will have thought, in other words, partly along natural-law lines, though by no means need he have done so in the over-systematized and dogmatic manner of some natural-law writers.

(I speak of judge rather than jury, because we assume that the jury deals with questions of fact rather than of law. But juries do sometimes decide on appraisal not only of fact but of felt equity. And the question formally of "fact" may contain a normative question; deciding whether a defendant was "negligent" entails deciding what constitutes negligence. In both ways the jury undoubtedly takes part in shaping law toward communal perceptions of justice.)

In its legislation, then, and in its judicial decisions, our positive law is suffused with natural-law thought in the general sense. There is here no question of an opposition between the two, much less of a radically antidemocratic suzerainty of natural law over positive law. Positive law, in a democratic society, admits just as much shaping toward ethical goals as the people desire. Their desire is expressed, as always, through their representatives. In this manner they have not only acted by legislation but also have left extensive and vital leeways in the technical framework of positive law, thus inevitably committing to their judicial representatives the task of filling the law out with such perceptions of justice as may be needful.

One level at which this process of suffusion operates is peculiar to our political system. Our Constitution, which controls other law, contains certain general provisions which stem from convictions as to the demands of justice: "due process of law," "equal protection of the laws," "freedom of speech," and others.

When a judge considers whether a certain procedural innovation offends against "due process of law," he may find—in historical documents, in past decisions, in other technical materials—a clear preponderance of evidence on one side of the question. If this happens, then he has no honest alternative to deciding the case accordingly. But if, as often occurs, the technical materials do not settle the question, then the judge must decide in obedience to his convictions as to the consonance of the new statute with the root principles of procedural fairness which he believes to be embodied in the words of the Constitution.

In this limited but important sense a component of what may be called "natural law" not only enters—as we have already seen—into the whole fabric of law at ordinary levels but also controls and even negates ordinary law. This happens not because "natural law" has any validity as law in itself. It happens because the American people in their basic juristic act—the putting and keeping in force of their Constitution—have chosen to embody in its words such principles as seemed good to them of what they have taken to be natural justice, leaving it to the courts to work out the application of these principles to concrete cases.

The American legal system, then, has rejected, as it should, the notion of a "natural law" standing outside positive law and dictating to the latter. But it has not for that reason fallen into the opposite error of proclaiming that mere legality is enough—that whatever is, is right. It has made a simple but most fruitful and creative synthesis. It has built into itself, as a positive-law system, abundant means of growth toward right law. The leeways are not ideally distributed; the controls are not perfect. Their effectiveness is altogether dependent on the qualities of mind and character of those who work in law. But I venture to say that no better solution has yet been devised to the problem of relating the positive law, the law that actually is, to the law of vision, the ideal law, the law that some have seen as implicit in the nature of man.

I want to conclude with a thought which—like the rest of this article—will doubtless be unsatisfactory or even objectionable both to those who hold natural law in scorn and to its earnest devotees. I will get at it by telling a true story. One afternoon last fall I was on my way to my class in Constitutional Law. I was going to lead a discussion of certain technicalities having to do with the application of the Fourteenth Amendment, as implemented by acts of Congress, to voting and other rights. My head was full of section numbers in the Federal Revised Statutes. I fear I was mumbling to myself, a practice I cannot recommend to those who hold reputation dear.

I happened to look up—all the way up, over the tops of the red stone buildings into the sky as the Indians of Connecticut must have seen it before the white settlers came, with its great autumnal castles of clouds as far as imagination could reach. And somehow, very suddenly, all this illimitable expansiveness and lofty freedom connected within me with the words I was tracing from the Fourteenth Amendment through the statute books—"privileges or immunities of citizens," "due process of law," "equal protection of the laws." And I was caught for a moment by the feeling of a Commonwealth in which these words had not the narrow, culture-bound, relative meaning we are able to give them in the "real" world, but were grown to the vastness that is germinal within them.

I went to my class with a different view toward the day's work. Not that I abandoned present technicalities and made a speech about alabaster cities. Far from it! The class was the most narrowly technical I had taught during the year. A musician who hears an unworldly music on his way to the concert hall must surely respond, if he is a musician, not by relying on his feelings when he gets up to play, but by being especially attentive to the accuracy of his tempo.

Nor did I go on believing that, if only we all worked hard enough in law, that Commonwealth in the clouds would come down to earth. No, the Heavenly City is where it may be, and our earthly cities will always be dirty and full of noise.

But I walked toward my technicalities somehow sure that, though the work of law in society can never be lightened or its incertitudes smoothed away by the vision of perfect liberating justice, and though all the work we do can never come within far galactic distance of bringing the vision to our life, still it is the vision that gives to the work the best value it possesses. I do not know exactly how this may be; the clearest thought I have about it is that all our work in law may be a ritual, celebrating the vision, assuring that while it can never be wholly found, it can never be wholly lost.

Law in latter days has gained much in realism, in hardheadedness, in disdain for orotundity and rhetorical glitter. This gain, like all gains, comes with its built-in peril—in this case the deadly peril of loss of the poetry of law. The poetry of law solves no legal problems; it was, in fact, brought into disrepute precisely by misbegotten attempts to make it solve legal problems—and herein all known schools of "natural law" have offended. The poetry of law is the motive for solving problems, the sacred stir toward justice, our priceless discontent at the remoteness of perfect law. The natural-law tradition, however irritating may have been its bumptious attempts to sell us its figmental street maps of the Heavenly City, has at least tried to keep the poetry of law alive.

Herein lies the clue, it seems to me, to our best utilization of the work that the natural-law thinkers, in all their schools, have done. We must first separate their poetry from their prose and then face the fact that the prose states no eternal, infallible truths, but only tentative conclusions, reasoned well or ill, about practical problems. There is no "anti-intellectualism" in believing that our minds are not made to ascertain beyond doubt the content of an immutable justice; one of the most precise and subtle uses of the intellect is in marking its own limits. Once through this realistic wringer, the prose component in each of the great natural-law constructions would surely have much to contribute, by way of fruitful insight and hypothesis, to the quest for justice.

The poetry, on the other hand, solves nothing, decides nothing, conveys no information, weighs nothing on the scale of argument. It is too precious for those uses. It may assure us, if we keep still and listen, that the whole business of decision, of argument, of long and disappointing search for information and solution, is after all worthwhile.

TALISMANIC NAMES AND
MODERN JUSTICE*

I think I shall begin by repeating, substantially, what I said on a recent similar occasion at my old University in Austin. I know that the conventional thing for me to speak of at such a time as this is my feeling of humility. The trouble is that I have never been in active politics, and so do not find the expression of humility as easy—as nearly automatic—as it is to those men in political life who so continually assure us how humble they feel. One often wonders how people so prone to humility got into politics in the first place. For my part, just now I feel too pleased with this honor to be humble. I understand the administration here had some trouble finding academic headgear large enough to fit me today. Let me be humble tomorrow; today I am proud and grateful.

"Let's kill all the lawyers!"

These words, put by Shakespeare into the mouth of a turbulent confederate of Jack Cade, are often quoted as if coming from the Bard himself, and as expressing, if not his literal wish, far less his literal intention, at least his evaluation of the worth of us and of our calling—yours and mine—an evaluation scarcely in the complimentary range.

Now, you are going to be lawyers; you already are lawyers. I can prophesy with entire confidence that not on one but on very many occasions you will be challenged fundamentally as to

*Address on Receiving Honorable Degree of Doctor of Laws from Boston University, 1 June 1975.

the worth of our profession and its work. This often happens at cocktail parties, for example, as the martinis follow one another down the aesophagi in attendance; the expressions, by people not always as far gone in political passion as Dick Butcher in *Henry VI, Part 2,* are correspondingly more moderate, but you will be given to understand, sometimes condescendingly, sometimes angrily, that we lawyers are, after all, of those "Who feed where desolation first has fed," and are really of no account and do no good, unless it be to make enough money to educate our children for something better.

I want first, therefore, to give you three talismanic names. Say these names to the top-loftiest cocktail-party assailant against our profession. Just say the names, then pause to give a little time for thought. If the person you are talking with is worth talking with at all, you won't have to say anything else. Let me pronounce these names to you slowly, in the order of their births and deaths: St. Thomas More, Abraham Lincoln, Mohandas K. Gandhi.

I give you these names, these particular names, because these men were not people who happened to be lawyers, and who were great at something else. Many names of this latter kind occur: Thomas Jefferson, Franklin Roosevelt, Wallace Stevens. But More, Lincoln and Gandhi were lawyers in their greatness as well as in their education and livelihood. Each of them was, to be sure, a thorough-paced professional lawyer, who earned his bread in our calling. But, more than that, each of them, in his times of highest greatness, thought his way like a lawyer to the positions he took and for which, in all three cases, I think one may say, he gave his life. Even the civil disobedience movement of Gandhi was obviously thought through in lawyer-like detail, and was executed with lawyer-like precision, with attention to legalistic niceties of distinction of just the sort that make those who are not lawyers so impatient with us who are.

St. Thomas More, Abraham Lincoln, Mohandas Gandhi. If your assailant is not ready to retire, give him five minutes to

match those names, for disinterested greatness, for nobility
linked to genius, with any three other names in the history of
the English-speaking world.

So, as to those self-doubters among us—and I am sometimes one of these—let me commend these names. We need
nothing to remind us that we can be pettifoggers, time-servers,
quibblers, experts in the "perfectly legal"—a phrase which has
come to connote dishonesty or overreaching just well enough
contrived to be shielded by the law's letter. But there remain
always St. Thomas More, Abraham Lincoln, and Mohandas
Gandhi. A painter can be a commercial artist for chewing-gum
ads. But Michelangelo was a painter too.

Law is the art of governing the human world. Being an art
of this generality, it has many tasks to perform. No one has
written of these to more effect than Karl Llewellyn, who identified these tasks as the resolution of conflicts, the setting up of
arrangements to avoid conflict, the allocation of jurisdiction,
the organization of society as a whole so as to enable it to move
toward larger goals, and the all-important devising of *methods,*
varying as these do from nation to nation and from time to time,
for accomplishing these four tasks of substance. Whichever of
these tasks is in focus at any one hour, the haunting goal above
all goals is the last beauty toward which the art of law can
reach—justice.

Many have asked "What is justice?" No answer, in words,
has the ring of true coin. Edmund Cahn suggested another form
the inquiry might take; we might ask, instead, "What is *injustice?*" Or rather, perhaps (for no general answer is attainable
here, any more than in the case of the affirmative question) we
may from time to time, from century to century, ask ourselves,
"Where, now, does *injustice* seem to be located? What, in this
society, are the most glaring injustices?"

Even when the inquiry is so limited by rephrasing, we cannot provide either mathematically or scientifically demonstrable
answers. Cahn called his chief work "The Sense of Injustice"; I

think that, having sharpened and purified our intellects, so as to see as deeply as possible into causes and consequences, into principles and their corollaries, we must at last take the leap, and trust our *sense* of injustice. And on what he senses as injustice the lawyer's radar ought to lock as the radar of the night-fighter plane locks on the unseen enemy aircraft.

I am going to talk to you a little on my own sense of the location of injustice in our society, in the hope not that you will accept blindly what I have to say, but that you will be led to form and sharpen your own radar systems. I know you all have livings to make. But so did Abraham Lincoln. His time came—his time to cease from being a skilled and faithful railroad lawyer. Yours will come also, if you keep awake for it.

The first remark I would make about injustice in America is that we have, doubtless through shame, always tried to shy away from its most conspicuous and altogether dominant manifestation. Other nations have other histories, and injustice is multifarious. But we have our very specific history, and that history exhibits not only, here and there, injustice in all its possible forms, but the overwhelmingly preponderant injustice of racism. Our history is built around racism, from the massive horror of slavery and its sequels, through the smaller-scaled but in some ways even more cold-bloodedly horrible massacres of American Indians who got in the way, down to all the picayune, but in the aggregate psychologically and economically mutilating racial injustices of times very fresh in my own memory. Generalities about injustices are mere evasions of the central truth about *our* injustice. *Hamlet* was not a philosophical tract on indecision; it was a play about a particular young Danish prince. Injustice in America has not been an abstraction, or a miscellany without theme; it has centrally concerned racism. (I add here parenthetically, for now, that I have not forgotten the injustice of sexual discrimination, which stretches over all the world and through all human time on earth.)

I am led at this point to several observations. I will begin one with a true story. Last fall, I was with some students at the University of Texas in Austin. These young people were mixed black and white, associating together in a public place on easy terms, as is altogether expectable in Austin now. Somehow the talk turned to the racial situation in Austin in my own student days. I told them that a gathering such as the present one was in those days quite impossible, that it would probably have raised a mob, and that at the least the police would have intervened, because we were in a place of public resort, where service to black and white together was flatly illegal. I told them that not only would the blacks not have been at the University of Texas, but that there was not within five hundred miles any college of remotely comparable quality which they could have attended. As they questioned me, I went into other aspects of the subject. I told them, for example, about lynching. I told them that it was, in the Texas of my youth, barely acceptable for one to express oneself as being opposed to lynching, but that one had to be very careful how one spoke; it was *de rigeur,* as I remember, to add that of course "these people" would be convicted and executed, and even then the too-enthusiastic opponent of lynching ran some risk of being suspected of holding dangerous opinions on the whole subject of race. As to those dangerous opinions in general, I told them, their expression would bring, at best, ostracism from Austin white society, and could very possibly lead to one's suffering violence.

At about this point, I saw a certain look in their eyes, and I think I correctly interpreted that look. My interpretation thrilled me and gave me heart. For I could tell that they thought I was just making it all up, to pass the time with tall tales about old Texas. And that was thrilling to me because I saw that it all had worked—that the army in which, as a young fellow, I had enlisted for the duration, had so thoroughly conquered that nobody any longer believed in the enemy.

Of course Texas is not the world, and even Texas is far from perfect, in this as in so many other ways. I have no illusion—

far from it—that racism in the United States is conquered. It is very hard to strike a net balance as to evils not commensurable. But I can tell you two things for sure. The first is that anybody who does not believe that there has been immense, enormous improvement in at least the peripheral South, where millions of blacks live, just wasn't there and doesn't know what he is talking about. The second is that, so far as anyone can tell, this improvement came about through *law*, through the work of *lawyers*—in the *Brown* case, in the drafting of the Civil Rights Act of 1964, and throughout. There was nothing in the mere passage of time which made improvement inevitable. It took work—*legal* work.

The system I described to these young people seemed, forty years ago, to be of stern granite, built for the ages. The wisdom of the old folks, black as well as white, was that it would change, if at all, only in some unimaginably remote future. Forty years later, however much other evil may remain, *that* system is gone. I urge you to take heart from that. Don't listen to the old folks. Lock your radar on something as evil as the racist system I grew up within. The old folks may get a big surprise.

Whenever you are downhearted, remember a few dates. The very first hint of national protection of free speech, as against actions of the states, was in the *Gitlow* case, just fifty years ago; that happened because a lawyer, Walter Pollak, would not give up just because a contrary dictum had emanated from the Supreme Court a few years before. It has been less time than that— less than fifty years—since the Supreme Court reversed its very first state criminal conviction on the ground that a confession had been obtained by torture, actual torture. Law does change for the better, and in a short period sometimes, and always through the energy of lawyers. Let your radar scan.

Yet I would remind you that racism is very often implicated in these changes. For example, the elevation of due process standards in criminal cases has largely been occasioned by excesses having a racist motivation. The present fight against the death penalty, on grounds of its being administered without coherent standards and by mistake-prone means, goes on against the background of a 58% black population on death row, as against 11% in the population at large. And the highest injustice of our times—of your young time—is really an injustice into which racial injustice has become merged.

I refer, of course, to poverty. We have no right, in this country, to tolerate poverty. There is a strong reaction on the injustice radar every time the air-conditioned car drives past the shack with malnourished children inside. I say racism has become merged with this problem, overall, because black people are poor in a proportion far outside their proportion in the population, and I think that, though easily visible vestiges of the more forthright racist system remain, it is poverty that now chiefly oppresses blacks.

Yet it is politically and practically impossible—as I think it would be morally wrong—to move toward relieving black poverty without also relieving white poverty. Racism now chiefly expresses itself in black poverty, but at last the interests of black and white, always latently the same, have visibly merged.

I hope you lock your radars—some of you—on poverty. We older lawyers are obsolete for this work; it wants fresh concepts and fresh courage. Some years ago, I wrote a piece in which I said, thoughtlessly, that the work of eliminating the injustice of poverty was not for lawyers. Before the piece was reprinted, I thought better of it, and dropped a footnote stating my sober second thought, which was that good lawyers could manage anything. The work of dealing with poverty will require just that mastery of huge masses of fact, just that skill in draftsmanship, just that power of advocacy, just that capacity for bringing abstract scientific concepts down to earth and putting them to work, that belong to the lawyer and to nobody else. Above all, what is wanted is a disciplined though passionate hatred of injustice; to hate injustice, with discipline and passion, is our highest calling; with others it is an accident, with us it is of the essence.

You will notice that I have not mentioned courts as the scene of the coming fight against the injustice of poverty. I believe I can put my record up against anybody's as to advocacy of the vigorous use of the judicial power, where it has the weapons that are of avail. I think that the weapons of avail against poverty are in other hands, those of Congress and of our legislatures. Lawyers from time out of mind have worked within and for these bodies—they need us and we need them. I would be less than candid if I did not say that it seems to me that the courts, which have done and can do so much about due process, about freedom of expression, about overt racism, will not be able to play the principal part in the war against poverty, and against the racism now contained in and merged with poverty. But that is only how the matter appears to me. You, our leaders into the twenty-first century, are to be the competent and sufficient judges of this matter, and I will trust your decision, for I know it will be made with intelligence and honesty, from time to time, on the basis of an experience which will be yours, not mine.

As I have briefly indicated, there is in what I have said an omission of such size that I must give it the emphasis of the closing position. I mean, of course, the world-wide and history-long injustice to women, an injustice, or complex of injustices, even more deeply rooted, it may be, than racism. On this subject, it seems to me that both courts and legislative bodies have much to do—but again I would say that, in the main, the tools for dealing with this most ancient of injustices, insofar as law can deal with it, are in legislative hands—adding, again, that future judgment on all this will be up to you.

May you be aware of being blest in the very seriousness of all this work. May you not be discouraged on learning that "justice" is a word like "eastward," marking a direction of movement and not a point that can be reached—or on learning that there are no compasses, only a few stars far more often than not hidden by clouds. And may you be strengthened much by laughter and all happiness.

COMMENCEMENT ADDRESS, THE STORM KING SCHOOL*

Today you are graduating from the Storm King School. I am going to tell you a secret, a secret I have carefully guarded from the Headmaster. Today is also Graduation Day for me.

I have for many years been a member of a large class, from which comparatively few ever graduate. I refer, of course, to the class composed of those who have never made a Commencement Day address.

There were many interesting people in this class. In a way, I hate to leave them. Besides that, I face my graduation with some of the dread we all feel when we go forth into the unknown. I haven't any idea what it will be like to be a person who has delivered a commencement address. Like you, then, I look with mixed emotions on the fact that today is my graduation day, and this is my valedictory.

Now, although I have never before delivered a graduation address, I have listened to one. The giving of such addresses is a very old custom, and one was delivered when I graduated from the high school in Austin, Texas. Surprising as it may seem, I even remember a little bit about it.

The speaker was a former Governor of Texas. He spoke in a practiced manner which made it very clear that he was by no means delivering his first such talk. The speech was full of alliteration. As I recall, he compared the pomp and pride of purple

*Delivered 7 June 1958. Reprinted from *The Occasions of Justice* by Charles L. Black, Jr. New York: The Macmillan Company, 1963. Copyright Charles L. Black, Jr. 1958.

passion with the mild though majestic meekness of manly modesty, expressing a preference for the latter. He contrasted the lolling limbs of the lily-livered lackadaisical loafer with the high-held head of the hale-hearted healthy-minded hero, and this made me wince, for I was afraid I recognized myself all too clearly under the first of these descriptions.

And he gave us advice—quite a lot of it, as I recall, though I am ashamed to say I don't remember anything very exact about it.

That was the last school graduation I attended. I know that times have changed. I do not know whether the custom of giving advice is one to which people in my present position still conform. I hope not. Advice, to me, is something to be given very rarely and with great hesitation, to someone you know very well. And I cannot think of a more impudent thing than for me to come here, after you have enjoyed for years the intimate personal guidance given by the able and devoted masters of this school, and to attempt in a few generalities to set you on the right track.

That is why I began by telling you my secret. I am sure you will not expect advice from one who is himself in the process of graduation. We are all facing a profound change. This is no time for us to give one another advice. It *is* a time, I think, for looking around us and sharing our observations about the world.

I can sum up my impressions down to now by saying that to me the world is a place of contradiction and mystery. Notice that I do not say "confusion." There is, to be sure, plenty of that. But confusion is something the mind can tackle, and make progress against if not dispel. Confusion is a road sign that is hard to read.

Contradiction is two very clear road signs pointing in opposite directions. And the clearer the contradiction, the deeper the mystery.

Life and the world seem to me to be founded on contradiction, and rooted in mystery. Examples rush to the mind from everything and from everywhere. I am going to select a few to talk about today because they happen to concern contradictions which were bothering me a great deal at just about the time of my own graduation from Austin High. I find them still freshly puzzling. I think people will worry about them for a long time to come.

When we start to look at the world, in order to find out something of the truth about it, we must, if we are at all thoughtful, begin to wonder a little about the notion of truth itself. To put the question in a short form used by many people, What is the nature of truth? If we have no clear idea about this, we seem to be in a pretty bad way for going on to find out the truth about some particular thing.

Now, one point seems obvious at once. If we are to see anything clearly, or reason about it correctly, we must look at things as they are—not as we would like them to be, or as pre-conceived ideas might lead us to expect them to be. Truth must be something outside our wishes and notions. Facts are facts, whatever we may think about them. This is sheer common sense, too obvious to need laboring. So we have put our hands on something solid.

But I'm sure you will already have seen the contradiction, which is equally a matter of common sense. We can't see anything except through our own eyes. We can't think about anything except with our own minds. What we call "truth" can never possibly be anything more than what we, with our imperfect senses and limited mental powers, accept as true at some particular time. We cannot jump outside this limitation anymore than we can jump out of our own skins.

Truth, then, is impersonal, or it is not truth. But truth is also personal, or we can't talk about it at all or have any ideas at all about it. The road signs are pointing in different directions. I don't know how the contradiction can be resolved; it is enough for now to say that the philosophers who have tried to resolve it have been entirely unsuccessful in agreeing among themselves. Let's pass on to something else.

Every intelligent person must ponder, from time to time, the problem that goes by the name of "freedom of the will." As I say this, I feel homesick for another time and place, because this is a problem which intensely concerned me in those warm spring days in Texas just before my graduation. Are all our thoughts and actions dictated by the working of causal laws, or do we actually have the power to make free choices uncompelled by the force of causation?

There could hardly be any question more absolutely basic to an estimate of what it means to be human.

Now, it is obvious that, if we are going to try to understand ourselves and other people, we have to proceed on the assumption that thoughts and actions have causes. To say, "He asked Sadie Brown to go to the dance because he chose to," is to explain nothing. We immediately ask, "But why did he choose to?" And this leads to a discussion which makes sense only as long as it goes forward in terms of cause and effect. So if we are to make human beings intelligible, if we are to talk coherently about their actions and thoughts, we must assume that these actions and thoughts are governed by causal laws.

But of course the contradiction arises. Life simply cannot be lived if we do not make the assumption that, when we feel ourselves free to choose which piece of candy to take or which girl to marry, this feeling of freedom is a valid feeling. Try it for an hour some time. Tell yourself: "I am a mere automaton. I will make no choices, because choice is just an illusion. I will allow myself to be operated by the laws of cause and effect." I think you'll find the experiment quite impossible to perform. But even if you don't, it will have failed anyway, because you decided to perform it and to stick with it—a succession of choices.

So human life is unintelligible or unlivable, depending on whether you affirm or deny the so-called "freedom of the will."

These contradictions and others like them are fundamental. They concern the deepest of our assumptions about life. But, like many good things, they can get a little filling, so let's go on to some matters more immediately involved in our everyday living.

Is a man to look for his values, for the working out of his salvation, in himself or in his society—as an individual or as a member of a team?

Man has no real existence except in association with others. His speech, his thoughts, his habits, his diet, his loves and his hates, his pride and his shame—all are learned from other people or arise from reactions to other people. To consider man apart from society is like considering a stream apart from the bed in which it flows. It isn't a stream anymore. All of man's life is geared into the lives of others, and all his values, all the good things he can seek, must be located in his relations with other people. This makes sense.

It also makes sense to say that every man is and must be utterly alone. He can never directly share his thoughts or feelings. He can make noises and gestures, which may stimulate in other people thoughts and feelings roughly similar to his own thoughts and feelings. But these are themselves locked up in him, and the lock has no key. *His* love and *his* hate are within him, and it is only as an individual that he can hope to find peace or happiness.

Taken by itself, each of these lines of thought is convincing. Set face to face, they are at war. And I can suggest no terms of truce.

I'll introduce a final contradiction by telling you of something I heard on the radio the other day. A well-known novelist was being interviewed. He said, "Life is either a tragedy or it's worth living; you have to make up your mind which." This man saw a simple choice. The world is either a good place or it is a bad place: Check one. When I heard that sentence, I decided I wouldn't bother to read any of his books. I can't think there would be anything very profound in the work of a man who thought he had to choose, or could choose, between these alternatives.

Of course life is a tragedy, and the world is a bad place indeed. I don't think you'll need me to summarize the evidence of this statement; it is obvious and overwhelming. It is in the headlines and on the back pages, in the eyes of strangers and in the confidences of people we know.

And of course the world is a good place, a very good place indeed. Here again I see no need to bring forward the over-powering evidence. It, too, is all around us, in the things we enjoy, in the knowledge we can win, in the beauty we can appreciate, in the work we can do, in the people we love and will love.

The world, then, is a bad place, a place of disaster and shock and ugliness and trouble. The world is a good place, a place of as much goodness and beauty as we can endure. The signs are pointing in opposite directions. And the mystery is one of the deepest we know.

Let me make it very clear that I am not playing a game with you today. These contradictions, and the many others that confront us when we look at life and the world, are utterly real to me. I have not resolved them, I have not cleared up the mystery that underlies them, and I see no hope that I ever will. And, like you, I am annoyed and sometimes even agonized by them. I don't expect the world to be simple. But I wish that it would make sense. Or so I think, sometimes.

Then I try to imagine a different kind of world, a world without contradiction or mystery. In such a world, the nature of truth would, in some way, be entirely clear. Our own natures would be perfectly understandable—no puzzles about "free will" or anything of the sort. Problems about the conduct of individual and social life would be problems in detail only, for the proper basic principles would be well understood. And this world would be either good or bad, not a world that can at one moment set us raging at its insensate cruelty and at another fill us with thankfulness that we are alive.

But as I try to build such a world in my imagination, I

realize that I am strangely repelled by it. And I soon locate the trouble: There are no people in it. There are beings of some kind—gods or machines—but no real people. And so you and I would have no place there. And I don't think we would want to be there.

Maybe we'd better content ourselves with being human. "Content" is doubtless too weak a word, for the business of being human is an exciting one indeed, if we see that it consists in the taking on of a set of jobs, defined by the contradictions I have been exploring. To be fully human is to search with passion and sacrifice for truth, for the cool truth that is true whatever anyone may think, and at the same time to be able to laugh wryly at the inevitable fact that the only truth we know anything about is what *we* think is true. It is to behave responsibly, as persons with power to choose our own course, not because we *know* we are responsible—that would be rather easy—but to behave responsibly without knowing whether we are responsible or not. It is to live to the fullest measure both in the society that is the essence of humanity and in the loneliness that is the essence of humanity, somehow trying to treat each as though it were everything. It is to hate the world for what it is, and to love the world for what it is.

Underlying all these contradictions is the greatest mystery of all: *Why?* I don't know, anymore than you do. It has occurred to me, as I am sure it must have occurred to you, that it may all be some kind of test.

I have just about graduated now, and you will shortly do so. I don't know what life is like in the class of those who have made Commencement Day addresses, but it won't take me long to find out. You too will move on into a different category, and go into many kinds of study and work. Perhaps some evening one of you will look at himself in the mirror and say, with wonderment, "Today I was asked to deliver a talk to the graduating class at a fine school." If that happens to you, I know you'll understand then, as perhaps you already do, why I feel this to be a special occasion for me as well as for you, and why I have felt so honored at having had this chance to talk to you.

Good luck, success, and happiness!

MY WORLD WITH
LOUIS ARMSTRONG*

In the middle of May 1955, at the Savoy Ballroom on Lenox
Avenue in Harlem, a philanthropic organization in the black
community gave a reception in honor of the thirty or so lawyers
who had worked on the case of *Brown v. Board of Education,* the
1954 Supreme Court decision that declared school segregation
unlawful and thus began the end of the old Southern racist
regime. I, by the grace of somebody or something, was there.
Thurgood lined us all up in front of the orchestra to receive the
applause of the whole crowd, Margaret Truman, Averell Harriman, everybody. I turned and looked, a little wistfully, at the
trumpet-player in the orchestra, a young black; "I wonder," I
thought, "whether I wouldn't rather have been honored in the
Savoy Ballroom for trumpet-playing?" Then I heard Thurgood,
moving down the line, ". . . Charlie Duncan. And next over
there is Charlie Black, a white man from Texas, who's been with
us all the way."

All the way. Yes, I guess so, if you can say that about something without beginning or end. I looked at Barbara, out at our
table; no knight reaching to take the garland of victory ever saw
eyes more glowing than hers as they fixed mine. We had been
married just over a year; the children were still waiting to be
born.

Then it was all over, Margaret Truman had to go, and Averell

**Yale Review,* Volume LXIX, Number One, Autumn 1979. Copyright Yale
University 1979. Thanks are due to the *Yale Review.*

Harriman, and we said goodbye to Charlie Duncan, and to Thurgood, and took a taxi back to our apartment at 300 West 109th Street, near Columbia, where I still taught, and where Barbara was just finishing Law School. We were quiet on the elevator, quiet into the vestibule, the living room. I went over to the record-player, and put on Louis's *Savoy Blues,* the 1927 Okeh. It was twenty-eight years old then; now it is fifty years old. I listened to it all through; Barbara stood silent behind me. When it was over, I stayed still a moment more, then I turned to her and said, "Well, baby, thank God, that's one thing I didn't go back on."

What did I mean by that? I don't entirely know; one never entirely knows the ways of the power of art. I know a little of the framework, a little of the rational components. But when these are exhausted, art remains inexhaustible, unknowable. But I do know that playing that one record, just then, for the sake of remembering, was the only right thing I could do.

I never met Louis, except for a couple of handshakes at the bandstand. Yet no first meeting in my life ever had the impact on me of my first encounter with him.

In September 1931, posters appeared in Austin advertising four dances, October 12 through 15, to be played by one "Louis Armstrong, King of the Trumpet, and His Orchestra," at the old Driskill Hotel. I was entirely ignorant of jazz, and had no idea who this King might be; hyperbole is the small coin of billboards. But a dance at the Driskill, with lots of girls there, was usually worth the seventy-five cents, so I went to the first one.

Memory is splotchy. I don't remember the moment or exactly the process of realization. But since that evening, October 12, 1931, Louis Armstrong has been a continuing presence in my life. Now, once a year—more than halfway into the fifth decade after that night, a senior professor who can hear retirement marching with audible heavy tread toward the 1931 University of Texas freshman—I present, in the Faculty Lounge

at the Yale Law School, what I call my "Armstrong evening"—
records of the 'twenties and early 'thirties. I have done this every
year since Louis died in 1971. As the students readily discern,
this is in truth a memorial service, a ritual of gratitude and
blessing for the soul of this man. My children come, if they
possibly can, dispersed as they are, for they understand. On the
day Louis died my David, then twelve and in summer camp,
wrote me a letter of condolence.

One way to describe the impression of that October night
is to say that Louis seemed—as was guessed, I believe, of
Paganini—under demonic possession—strengthened and
guided by a Daemon. Steamwhistle power, lyric grace, alter-
nated at will, even blended. Louis played mostly with his eyes
closed; just before he closed them they seemed to have ceased
to look outward, to have turned inward, to the world out of
which the music was to flow.

Years ago I published the lines:

And the musicians sit there, ending phrases
By that slight taking-in of breath. The blowing musician
Pushes out from fullness of thought. He stops. There is nothing
Left but himself, empty except of himself.
His eyes open, but his look is the look of a rock
That has done what it came to do, collects and remembers
Itself eternally. Naked into the world
His world blazed forth, it patterned the blank of darkness
With clean light-lines; it is, and he is himself
Only, taking breath, waiting to enter again.

By that time, I had seen Louis on many occasions, but I
think the lines were above all engendered by that first evening.

Louis was thirty-one when I first heard him, at the height
of his creativity. He was just then in the borderland between his
two greatest periods—the dazzlingly inventive small-band period of the Hot Five and Hot Seven, and the first period of
improvisation around popular melodies—*Stardust, Chinatown,
When Your Lover Has Gone.* All through these years, he was let-

ting flow, from that inner space of music, things that had never before existed.

He was the first genius I had ever seen. That may be a structurable part of the process that led me to the Brown case. The moment of first being, and knowing oneself to be, in the presence of genius, is a solemn moment; it is perhaps the moment of final and indelible perception of man's utter transcendence of all else created. It is impossible to overstate the significance of a sixteen-year-old Southern boy's seeing genius, for the first time, in a black. We literally never saw a black, then, in any but a servant's capacity. There were of course black professionals and intellectuals in Austin, as one later learned, but they kept to themselves, out back of town, no doubt shunning humiliation. I liked most of the blacks I knew; I loved a few of them—like old Buck Green, born and raised a slave, who still plays the harmonica through my mouth, having taught me when he was seventy-five and I was ten. Some were honored and venerated, in that paradoxical white-Southern way—Buck Green again comes to mind. But genius—fine control over total power, all height and depth, forever and ever? It had simply never entered my mind, for confirming or denying in conjecture, that I would see this for the first time in a black man. You don't get over that. You stay young awhile longer, with the hesitations, the incertitudes, the half-obedience to crowd-pressure, of the young. But you don't forget. The lies reel, and contradict one another, and simper in silliness, and fade into shadow. But the seen truth remains. And if this was true, what happened to the rest of it?

That October night, I was standing in the crowd with a "good old boy" from Austin High. We listened together for a long time. Then he turned to me, shook his head as if clearing it—as I'm sure he was—of an unacceptable though vague thought, and pronounced the judgment of the time and place: "After all, he's nothing but a God damn nigger!"

The good old boy did not await, perhaps fearing, reply. He walked one way and I the other. Through many years now, I

have felt that it was just then that I started walking toward the
Brown case, where I belonged. I realized what it was that was
being denied and rejected in the utterance I have quoted, and I
realized, repeatedly and with growingly solid conviction
through the next few years, that the rejection was inevitable, if
the premises of my childhood world were to be seen as right,
and that, for me, this must mean that those premises were
wrong, because I could not and would not make the rejection.
Every person of decency in the South of those days must have
had some doubts about racism, and I had had mine even then—
perhaps more than most others. But Louis opened my eyes
wide, and put to me a choice. Blacks, the saying went, were "all
right in their place." What was the "place" of such a man, and
of the people from which he sprung?

In the months and years just following, I avidly collected
Louis's records. In those days, the great old Okehs of the 'twenties were still in stock at the J.R. Reed Music Co. on Congress
Avenue, or could still be ordered from open-stock catalogs. You
paid seventy-five cents apiece for recordings by Jan Garber, Guy
Lombardo, and Rudy Vallee, but Louis, on Okeh—such titles
as *West End Blues, Knockin' a Jug, Tight Like That*, the *Savoy
Blues* wherein I heard a trumpet blowing for me—were to be
had for thirty-five cents each, being classified as "race records,"
though they were even then being eagerly collected by pink-
pigmented members of the human race in England and France.

I bought a lot of them, and have almost all of them yet.
They are still of surprising sonic quality, though some have
surely been played a thousand times. No material has ever been
quite as good, for records, as the material they used then, and
no engineers ever recorded Louis quite as well as the Okeh engineers did. I play them at my annual service; the students,
understandably, had rather hear and even see them than listen
to tapes.

I falter when I turn to describing these records. Music cannot be written about directly—not the feeling part of it. Yes,

Skip the Gutter has a dialogue, on trumpet and piano, between Louis and Earl Hines, that is the finest example I know of the musical sense of humor—the sense of humor purely musical, in that it uses no trick effects, no barnyard "imitations," but sticks to clean musical technique alone—Olympian laughter. Yes, *Mahogany Hall Stomp* illustrates supremely well that quality of inevitability that so often marks great music—it must have been just so, and in no other way, though who would have thought of it? Yes, *Knee Drops* is a cascade of bluish diamonds. Yes, *West End Blues* (like dozens of others of these records) sets the mind wondering how people could have heard this jazz as only "hot"— whorehouse music almost—when so much of it is quiet, stately chamber music. Yes, one has sat, so many years later, in a pub in Birmingham in England, with a bassoonist on the University music faculty there, a man good enough to have played with Dennis Brain before arthritis impeded his fingering, listening to him talk about the two marvelous conversations Louis holds with his horn about the melody, on the two 1930 masters of *Stardust*.

But this is just talk. You have to listen to these records. They do not date. I listened to them all, over and over and over again. And now it was not a matter of shock-impact, but of slow and thorough realization, of living oneself into the work of an artist. There have been many—well, a good many—great artists in my time. But it just happened that the one who said the most to me—the most of gaiety, the most of sadness, the most of high nervous excitement, the most of religion-in-art, the most of home, the most of that strange square-root-of-minus-one world of emotions without name—was and is Louis. The artist who has played this part in my life was black.

In 1957, in the early days after the Brown case, when the South was still resisting, I wrote out and published my deepest thought on the nature of the agony as it presented itself:

I'm going to close by telling of a dream that has formed itself through the years as I, a Southern white by birth and training, have pondered my relations with the many Negroes of Southern origin that I have known, both in the North and at home.

I have noted again and again how often we laugh at the same things, how often we pronounce the same words the same way to the amusement of our hearers, judge character in the same frame of reference, mist up at the same kinds of music. I have exchanged "good evening" with a Negro stranger on a New Haven street, and then realized (from the way he said the words) that he and I derived this universal small-town custom from the same culture. I have seen my father standing at the window of his office with a Negro he had known for a long time, while they looked out on the town below and talked of buildings that used to be here and there when they were young.

These and thousands of other such things have brought me to see the whole caste system of the South, the whole complex net of its senseless cruelties and cripplings, as no mere accidental grotesquerie of history, but rather as that most hideous of errors, that *prima materia* of tragedy, the failure to recognize kinship. All men, to be sure, are kin, but Southern whites and Negroes are bound in a special bond. In a peculiar way, they are the same kind of people. They are happy alike, they are poor alike. Their strife is fratricidal, born of ignorance. And the tragedy itself has, of course, deepened the kinship; indeed it created it.

My dream is simply that sight will one day clear and that each of the participants will recognize the other.

Buck Green was in those words, and a kind girl who played with me when I was little, and Hugh Ledbetter ("Leadbelly"), whom I knew slightly and loved a great deal, and Harvey and Maggie Crayton, and Carlene Thomas and the incomparable Teddy Wilson, and both Jim Nabrits, and all my black companions-in-arms at law, and Frankie Newton, whose heart, I have always believed, broke from the strain of being black. Jack Teagarden is there too, I think, for from the little conversation and much music I had from him, I believe that he, also a white Texan, would have agreed. (Louis, I have learned, refused for a time to play in New Orleans because Teagarden, a member of his "All-Stars," could not play with him.) How many, many more!

But Louis has the special place of the artist of my time who uniquely instructed me, as only high art can instruct, on all the matters I have written of above, and who was black.

How could I have been anywhere else when the Brown case was moving up? By the time I got there, I had left behind the feeling that I was struggling for justice for somebody else. I was, in my own heart, in an army for and with my own.

But that doesn't quite reach the end of the inquiry with which I started. I came home from that party and played the *Savoy Blues*. Not another record. Just that one. Well, I must confess there was something more direct there. Perhaps it was and is only an imagination of mine. But in the trumpet on that record, just that one, I thought I heard something said—as a self-knowing high artist might say it—gently, without stridency or self-pity, perhaps with more pity for the more pitiable wrong-doer than for the wronged, but like this: "We are being wronged, grievously, heavily, bewilderingly wronged. We don't know why, or what to do. Is anyone listening? Is there anyone to come in and help us?" Then there is the gentle coda, a coda unmistakeably of resignation: "I leave it up to you."

Projection? More than likely. But great art invites projection, stimulates projection, cries, sometimes, for projection.

That is a little of what Louis has meant to me, and that is what I heard in his horn—so triumphant in other places and so full of glory—in the *Savoy Blues* of 1927. And again I thank God that that was one thing I didn't go back on. And for the miracle of art. And for Louis—may he be in peace.

REFLECTIONS ON READING
AND USING THE
CONSTITUTIONAL WORK OF
MAX GLUCKMAN*

In its beginning, I thought of this as an article for such lawyers as might pick up this volume. Its projected aim was to suggest to them—almost entirely by way of example—what value there might be in the study of work on tribal law, for the lawyer who wants to understand his own law better. I think it may have some interest to anthropologists too, for it may suggest to them a little of what we lawyers need.

I speak of "the study of work on tribal law," rather than of "the study of tribal law," because direct study of that law is not feasible for most of us. Such direct study is and has to be conducted in the field, by persons specially trained, persons thoroughly conversant with the language, culture and thought-modes of the tribal people whose law they are studying. It is true that the more general synthetists in this part of anthropology (and Max Gluckman was one of the greatest of these) must rely on the work of others, but they do so on the basis of an experienced understanding of the methods used, and hence can see more deeply—more operationally, if I may put it that way—into other anthropologists' accounts of law and law-like material. We lawyers do not, as lawyers, have that kind of training. Our intimate expertness is in our own law. We have to take

*Originally in *Cross-Examinations: Essays in Memory of Max Gluckman* edited by P. H. Gulliver. Leiden: E. J. Brill, 1978.

both the detailed findings and the higher syntheses on tribal law pretty much as they come to us, tentatively evaluating these mostly on the basis of suggestive value to us, rather than taking up our own positions on the intrinsic scientific worth of the material or on its fidelity to tribal institutions as they are.

For this value—very strictly speaking, more strictly speaking than any living person, with a full and healthy set of curiosities, is likely to be able to do—the rightness of the anthropological work is irrelevant. If an account of tribal law were to trigger a series of valuable insights into American law, and if these insights checked out in American law alone, then it would not matter at all, for that purpose, whether the depicted tribe even existed. Of course no one, subjectively, will be able to go that far in detachment from reality. But it is well to isolate this component in the non-tribal lawyer's use of tribal law material.

Let me give an example. Accounts of tribal law seem to exhibit at many points the use of divination to settle questions of fact. Chickens are eviscerated; the question of fact is settled by the state of the viscera. Bones are cast into the fire; the manner of their cracking answers the question.

The theoretical considerations underlying these practices are simple and eternal. Science and history do not have to answer any question of fact until cogent evidence is turned up; at this writing, we do not know whether there is life on Mars. I think it is true—to look at the historical side—that we do not really know whether Richard III murdered his nephews, though emotions set strongly in both directions. In such cases, it is entirely acceptable and indeed obligatory for the scientist or the historian to announce ignorance, and to wait till more evidence is developed before going farther.

The dispute-settling and order-keeping systems in society, on the other hand, stand under the pressing and continually self-renewing necessity of answering questions of fact which, on the evidence, *cannot confidently be answered*. "Did C commit adultery with Y?" "Did A threaten B with a knife, or not?"

Of course I am not saying that such questions are always inaccessible to rational answer. In any particular case, evidence may be available which, *mutatis mutandis,* would suffice for proving Martian life, to that high probability with which science commonly satisfies itself. What I am saying is that this very often is not so; cases must occur, in great numbers and in all societies, in which rational answer, on the basis of evidence, is not possible—cases as to which the scientist or historian would have to say, "I do not yet know, and may never know." Yet—unlike the question about life on Mars—the question about the knife *must* be answered, for answering it is an indispensable step in the settling of a real controversy that must and will in some way be settled. Put with more sophistication, the dispute-resolving organs of society must often behave *as if* some question of fact were resolved, though the scientific position as to that same question of fact would have to be that the evidence is insufficient for a rational answer. Emotionally, it is doubtful whether people at large can live with the sophistication of this *als ob*; such fully conscious inconclusiveness as to justice-in-fact would seem an unbearable strain. Whatever may be the case as to the latter point, the minimum certainty is that every society, whether or not it can bear admitting it, must have some means for settling on an authoritative and final answer to questions of fact which cannot rationally be answered.

Against this paradoxical background, divination can be seen as within the range of sensible solutions to a problem inherent in the dispute-settlement function. I need not expatiate on this obvious fact, but pass on to modern American law. What devices do we use for producing an authoritative answer—an answer to be acted upon—to questions of fact which a scientist would have to say are not answerable on the evidence? There are several, but the mind goes at once to the jury.

Here we have a curious confirmatory fact. The aim of our use of the jury in civil cases is that the jury be given just those questions to which no confident answer can be given on the evidence. If there is strong evidence—several eyewitnesses—to the effect that the plaintiff who was struck by an automobile was crossing the street against a red light, and there is no evidence to the contrary, the judge will commonly take that question away from the jury, for only one rational answer is possible on the evidence. If one witness testifies that it was green, and another that it was red, then, ordinarily, the question will go to the jury—precisely because the evidence does not settle it. It is striking what this procedure implies as to our real faith in the jury's reliability; we herein act on the supposition that the jury cannot be trusted to register the obviously right conclusion, while at the same time we confide to the jury questions which the evidence leaves dubious. (This account simplifies the use of the civil jury, but it is accurate for very many cases, and stresses that use of the jury toward which modern American civil procedure strongly tends.)

Is the jury, then, to be looked on as a form of divination? The function—that of answering a scientifically and even rationally unanswerable question—puts the jury in the divinatory range. But there are other suggestive resonances. The jury deliberates in guarded secrecy; investigation of its workings is frowned upon and made difficult. Each jury is assembled for one occasion only, so that the development of expertness in fact-finding is impossible. Absent gross misconduct, the jury is not in any way accountable or responsible; often spoken of as "democratic," it is in fact quite freed of the ordinary checks of democracy. There is a strong element of chance in the process; though its apologists speak of the jury as a "cross-section" of the community, no criminal defendant or other litigant has any right that it be an accurate "cross-section," but only that it not be so chosen as to *ensure* bias in certain regards. As a most dramatic example, a defendant on trial for his life has a right, in the United States, that persons who oppose the death penalty not be excluded from the jury, if the chance of the draw turns one or more of them up, but if the chance of the draw does not turn one of them up, he has no right to a jury that is a proportionally representative "cross-section of the community," with respect to what is for him an absolutely vital issue. There is ordinarily no way of checking the accuracy of the jury's verdict, for the "facts" are not (and *ex hypothesi* cannot be) "correctly" ascertained *aliunde*. It is hard to validate the assertion (which I feel intuitively to contain truth) that a vague feeling of divine guidance is present in the pro-jury apologetic; what is certain is that an almost equally mystical and entirely unsubstantiated folk-wisdom is commonly predicated of the jury.

One might also note that trial judges—who have to "find the facts" when a jury is not employed—are often the most articulate and impassioned defenders of the jury system. When officials are heard to favor the withholding of power from themselves, some explanation is called for. In this case, the explanation seems clear. The continual, day-to-day resolution of questions of fact which cannot be resolved rationally must be an immense strain; the judge, trained to rationality, must switch to intuition and even guessing; he must often rely—as must the jury—on the process of evaluating what is called, pretentiously, "demeanor evidence," which, writ plain, is neither more nor less than judging whether someone is lying by looking at him as he speaks—a manifestly and grossly defective mode of reaching truth. It is natural that any trial judge should desire to say to such a function, "Far be thou from me!"

Whatever the answer, then, to the question whether the jury "is" a mode of divination, much about the jury is clarified by considering its working as analogous to the divinatory. And I proffer this example here because these suggestive insights about the modern jury have to stand on their own feet, and do not depend on the correctness of the tribal law material about divination, or on my correct understanding of it—though I would much doubt whether I would have come to see the jury as a divinatory mechanism without having read such work.

For another kind of use, we do have to make tentative ongoing acceptance of the veridical value of the tribal law work. One example, without detail, will suffice. From many tribal law sources there seems to emerge the generality that the regime of punishment—roughly, "criminal law"—depends for its rehabilitative efficacy on smallness of the group, with the personal knowledge and personal concern that smallness makes possible. I believe there has never in the history of the world been a criminal-law system which to any satisfactory degree attained this goal of rehabilitation, except in groups small enough for face-to-face, personal concern to be genuine. At the present crisis in our own punishment system, and in a time of growing realization of its virtually total failure as to rehabilitation, we ought to be assessing as insightfully as possible the tribal modes. We might derive some suggestions of promising functional substitutions for the face-to-face situation which we cannot attain. We may learn (or seem to learn) that rehabilitation is an unattainable goal in our society. But in any case, at this stage at least, we ought to be making the best assessment we can of the tribal law work that has seemed to succeed.

I carried about an interest in tribal law, as pictured in the anthropological literature, some fifteen years before I met Max Gluckman. But my admiration for his work, and the most fortunate fact that I had his close friendship (which, as all know, with him meant the opening of his mind) for twelve years, make it impossible for me to trace back of that work and that friendship the lines of anthropological influence which Max's work and conversation so transmuted as to make his influence, to this single native informant now testifying, the dominant one. To say this is of course to confess anthropological imbalance—even incompetence—but that confession is in my case redundant. My anxiety to be explicit arises from a desire to be faithful to the essence of Max's scholarship, and there could be no greater faithlessness to that scholarship than the implantation of any suggestion that tribal law can be or should be approached only *via* his work. Max was in the greatest rabbinical tradition: he saw himself as a living part of the process of continually growing knowledge—as standing in working relations with all significant predecessors, contemporaries, and successors, all of them about the same great work. He intimately knew everything ever written in his field, and he saw his own writing as part of an ongoing scholarly effort, wherein, and only wherein, he acted and reacted both greatly and generously. He would have been the first to insist that the value of the study of tribal law to modern working lawyers could be reached by many roads.

But Max Gluckman's work can be recommended as an excellent, if not uniquely excellent, door of approach to tribal law work. This is true for several reasons.

First, though he thoroughly covers the private-law system of one tribe, and touches the private-law systems of others, his emphasis is on *constitutive* law, including the law of judicial power and procedure; this is a particularly good place to start in tribal law, for it is precisely as to these basic institutional matters that tribal law is likely to differ, in its fundamental postulates, from our own—or perhaps, on a closer look, suggestively to resemble our own. The question whether some tribal law is law at all has occupied much attention. Gluckman deals with this question in a most thorough way.

Secondly, Gluckman very explicitly places his work in the whole historical line, and at the same time reads and replies to much of the work of younger people who are still writing and developing their own fresh insights. Thus one is led by him into the whole literature.

Thirdly (and this is most important to the lawyer who would profit from looking into tribal law) Gluckman quite consciously and expressly attempts links with modern law. He himself had substantial training as a law student.

In the course of his studies of African tribal constitutions, Gluckman attained to some remarkably productive and clear insights into the operation of constitutive rules. He saw, for example, that the rules of succession to the kingship, one of the most significant set of rules in the Barotse constitution, were ambiguous, or self-contradictory, as a set. Instead of throwing up his hands at this, as a mere example of intellectual insufficiency, he was able to trace the effects of these rule-characteristics, in rebellion.

Generalizing, one could say that the investigation of legal rules—including constitutional rules—is not exhausted when one has said all there is to say about their meaning (including possible vagueness or ambiguity) and has looked into the question whether the particular rule is, in its own terms, "obeyed." One must go further and consider what the dynamic consequences may be of the existence of just this rule, or just this set of rules. These are sometimes surprising, and go much wider than the literal tenor of the rule would suggest. In American constitutional law—as doubtless everywhere—this inquiry is essential to any serious evaluation of any rule.

For example, the effects of simple ambiguity or vagueness, often carelessly thought of as obvious defects, are sometimes seen on reflection and inquiry to be benign. The States of the Union are forbidden by the Constitution to make "any Agreement or Compact" with one another, without the consent of Congress. This seemingly comprehensive rule has been interpreted by the Supreme Court of the United States as not applying to "minor matters," such as boundary adjustment, so that the working rule of law is as vague as its key term—"minor matters." What could be sloppier? Yet the resulting vagueness probably has a good effect. If compacting States want to be absolutely sure of themselves, the consent of Congress will be sought and obtained. But at the same time, in any matter even arguably "minor," no State can feel quite sure it is not bound by an agreement it has made, even without congressional consent.

This is a small matter. Of far greater significance are some of the dynamic results of our basic constitutional rules for selection and empowerment of officers.

The fundamental power balance of the political departments—Congress and the Presidency—is not at all revealed in the written text of the Constitution. It is the *reaction* to the structures set up by that text that has given definite shape to the working government. This shape, being reactive-to-rule rather than rule-imposed, may change without the rules being broken, but it is hard to see what direction change is likely to take.

Virtually all the significant powers in the national government are given by the text to *Congress*. The power to regulate commerce, the taxing power, the power to declare war, to raise military forces, to enact rules for the governance of these, to deal comprehensively with property belonging to the government, and to appropriate money—all these powers are placed in Congress' hands, and as their scope has been interpreted by the Supreme Court, they add up to virtually plenary power over everything.

The President, on the other hand, is given astonishingly little power over matters of policy. He has been spoken of as the "sole organ" of the United States in foreign affairs, but the Constitution cannot, I think, be said even to hint at such primacy, since it places the President's treatymaking power under the shadow of the Senate (which must approve any treaty, before it can be valid, by a two-thirds majority), since it places the war-declaring power in Congress, and since it gives Congress unlimited and sole power to regulate commerce with foreign nations. The President cannot even appoint an ambassador without Senatorial approval, and of course all his actions and all his undertakings with respect to foreign affairs, if they are to be meaningful at all, must be supported by congressionally appropriated money, and by other affirmative congressional action.

The mere reading of the text of the Constitution would, then, easily lead to the conclusion that virtually all power in the American government was to be in the hands of Congress. I have not forgotten the veto power. But a Congress resolute on taking up and holding the leadership position in the American government could have disposed of the veto, as a practical matter, either by attaching the measures it wanted passed to appropriation bills—especially to those appropriating money for the conduct of the Presidency—or by the development of a convention that vetoes were always to be overridden. This is by no means a preposterous suggestion of possibility, since this convention, above all others possible, would enhance the standing of Congress as an institution, and thus, indirectly, the standing of all its members in the long run.

These possibilities never became reality because the *structures* created by the Constitution were not suitable for such a development, but, rather, pushed strongly toward Presidential power.

Congress is composed of two Houses, equal in power, aside from certain special functions (ratification of treaties, confirmation of Presidential appointments to office) given to the Senate. This bicamerality is absolutely firm under the Constitution, and since Senators, like Representatives, are popularly elected for limited terms, no charge can be made (as with the House of Lords) that the principles of democracy are rawly contradicted by the Senate's remaining in power. The place of the Senate, moreover, is made uniquely safe by a special provision that no State may be deprived of its equal representation in the Senate without its own consent—quite aside from the fact that any constitutional amendment must be passed by two-thirds of the Senate as well as of the House, and by three-fourths of the States—a manifest impossibility as to any amendment cutting down the senatorial power of the less populous States.

There is a tendency for the two Houses to be organized by the same party, but this means even less than might be thought, because the constituencies crucially vary. A State like Alaska, with a population of about 300,000 (1970 Census) and with only *one member* in the House of Representatives, has the same number of Senators—two—as California, with a population of 20,000,000 and 43 Members of Congress. The difference is systematic. It brings it about that except when the interests of the thickly populated States and those of the thinly populated States coincide, there is no guarantee at all that the Senate and the House will develop simultaneous majorities around any measure. The organization and discipline in each House (such as it is or can be) is entirely separate from that in the other. "Congress" is now treated, commonly, as a singular noun, but, grammar aside, it must be plain that these two independent bodies, House and Senate, could hardly be expected to act together in such a consistent way as to form out of themselves, or to make subject to themselves, an ongoing coherent government.

But this bicamerality is really the lesser of the two obstacles to making of Congress a body that actually governs. The heart-difficulty lies in the relationship of the Congressman and the Senator to his own home constituency. The principle of organization is strictly geographic. Both Senators and Representatives must be residents of the State they represent. Congressmen (in the case of States having more than one) are elected from *districts,* and in practice no candidate will be seriously considered for nomination or election unless he resides in or near the district from which he is sent. Attempts at changing one's State or district are rare, and successful attempts exceedingly rare.

Simply seen and said, this system makes serious party discipline in either House virtually impossible; the "leaders" and "whips" swing their blows through water. The Congressman or Senator who satisfies the party leadership, but displeases his district or State, has been a good boy, but no more is seen of him in Washington. The Senator or Congressman who bucks the party leadership, but satisfies the special interests of his constituency, keeps coming back, whatever the leadership wants— and sooner or later what the leadership wants is to get along reasonably well with a member who is going to be there anyway, and vote.

It is not as simple as that. There are cross-cutting pressures and ties. (Here, too, one thinks of Gluckman's work, and of its roots in the work of Evans-Pritchard and other anthropologists.) The member who wants to *accomplish something* in Congress must work with the party leadership; if he wants to get his bill through committee and to the floor of the House, he will need to be thought of by the leadership as being reasonably cooperative on other matters, given the constituency pressures which all know to lie on him. It is only the member who cares about nothing except continual reelection—just *being* a Congressman—who can be wholly independent of the leadership, and regardful only to his constituency. Few public people, mercifully, want to make that little of their lives. But survival must dominate, and survival depends almost not at all on the party leadership, and almost entirely on the constituency—which, practically speaking, cannot be changed.

It would be a great mistake to think of all this as a matter of Congressmen and Senators habitually voting against their consciences in order to be reelected. The truth is much subtler—and, on reflection, much more expectable. What usually happens is that a happy match is found between the general philosophy of the Congressman and the views of the constituency. If the constituency is highly conservative on economic matters, it is likely to elect a Congressman (or Senator) who is himself highly conservative on economic matters, who therefore votes his own conscience and his constituency's views simultaneously, and who experiences his total dependence on his constituency as *emancipation* from party leadership pressures, rather than as *subjection* to the home vote. There are many accidental variations from this pattern, but it is quite obviously the normal point toward which the system tends to come. And this makes even more difficult—more impossible I should have said, if the adjective "impossible" admitted of degrees of comparison—the existence of effective national party discipline in Congress. For insofar as this constituency-representative match is found, the member who goes against the party leadership in order to survive in his own constituency very often can at the same time feel, rightly, that he is following his own conscience. (And to this of course must be added that all of us—whether Congress-men, academics or insurance salesmen—can in marginal or doubtful cases convince ourselves that the best thing for our-selves is, at the same time, the best thing.)

Now it may seem almost a miracle that this two-headed body, not in the last resort amenable to any effective party dis-cipline, can be brought to agreement on the generalities of stat-utes. Below that level of generality, Congress cannot be expected to operate as a governing body.

On the other hand (and few words need be spent on this) the Presidency is ideally structured for the making of fine-grained (or even medium-fine-grained) decisions on policy: that is to say, it is ideally structured for the ongoing conduct of government. Final authority is in one person at the top, with such organization and delegation, all down the line, as that person shall think good. The efficiency of such a branch of gov-ernment, and the consistency of its actions, will of course de-pend on the ability and on the prestige of the President, but all that structure can do has been done to make this branch a suit-able executant (and hence, as Gluckman so clearly saw, a *former*) of policy in governance.

What has been the result? It has been a continuous volun-tary transfer of power from Congress to the President, by formal delegation under loose standards, and by acquiescence amount-ing to delegation. Congress can say, in effect, that aircraft ought not to make too much noise, given all the circumstances. But who decides whether the Concorde is to land in the United States? William Coleman, Secretary of Transportation—a Pres-idential Cabinet officer in no way responsible to Congress. This example may seem trivial. Think, then, of Congress's part in the Viet Nam war. Predictably (from structure, though certainly not from constitutional text) Congress's one and only intervention in regard to that longest of our wars, until the bitter end, was the Tonkin Gulf Resolution, which was a sweeping delegation of power to the President.

In fact, by far the greatest part of the President's powers has come to him not out of the Constitution but by congressional delegation, under standards so vague that virtually the whole of concrete policy in regard to the particular subject must be presidentially formed.

This is (and, despite turmoils, seems likely to remain) the true working American constitution, on the highest level. Yet a jurisconsult might be able to give the correct *responsa* to all possible questions about the *rules* of American constitutional law, and still not even suspect that the working constitution stands as it does. The relevant inquiry is not what the constitutional rules *mean*; they are, in fact, few in number and for the most part unproblematic of interpretation. The real inquiry has to be (and this is plainly true, whether or not I am right in everything I have so far said), "What is and has been the *dynamic reaction* to these rules? What behavior have they *evoked*, out of the large set of merely logical possibilities? And what is it about these rules that caused them to evoke just this behavior?" Right or wrong, the short and simplified analysis I have just presented is a sketchy paradigm of the *kind* of understanding necessary, if one is to understand the working of constitutive rules—a working entirely unrevealed by mere explication of the rules themselves.

I have even gone so far as to conjecture that the working American constitution, just because of the necessities of the case, would have been much the same, even if the Constitution—the written document—had taken on form seemingly quite different from the one it took. As it stands, there are three major constitutive Articles—Article I for Congress, Article II for the Presidency, and Article III for the judiciary. It is my belief—and I have proffered this conjecture only because I think it helps us to see more deeply into the working constitution as it stands—that if the Constitution had ended with Article I, creating nothing but Congress along present lines, an executive branch and a judicial branch, neither differing greatly from what we actually have, would have been created by Congress. The Congress structured by Article I could not, for the reasons I have given, have formed out of itself a "government" on parliamentary lines. Yet there must be an executive branch of some kind; what alternative would Congress have to creating it? Once it was created, the very same causes which have in fact produced congressional delegation of power to the President would have operated, and much the same flow of power from Congress to the executive branch would have ensued. Or so it seems to me. Of course, there would have been differences in detail, and a large difference as to the prestige of the President. But as a matter of naked law and last-resort power, a Presidency created by Congress would not be critically more under the threat of congressional control than is a President who could, in next year's appropriations bill, be given enough money to hire one social secretary, but not enough to pay the electricity bill at the White House, and certainly not enough for one tourist-class air passage for the Secretary of State to go to Montreal.

Is this kind of thinking influenced by Gluckman? I know that is the way, or one of the ways, in which he thought and wrote about constitutive-law rules. He looked not only for their "meaning" but for the behavior they evoked or facilitated. Through twelve years of my trying to see deeper into the structure of the working American constitution, he and I had constant intellectual traffic; his works and his talk were much on my mind. I cannot pinpoint any concrete influence as to a single point. But I am very sure there was a pervasive influence—suggestive and confirmatory.

For another example, let us take the veto power. The "rules" about it are simple. But the reaction to and within those rules is very complex.

When the President and Congress are at loggerheads, as they have often lately been, the veto power redefines the whole task of Congress, from the very beginning. The job is no longer that of devising and passing legislation implementing what

Congress judges to be the best possible policy, for example, on energy. The job is rather that of passing a bill which comes as close as it can to implementing Congressional judgment, while getting past the veto. And the catch is that it is not and cannot be known just what it will take to get past the veto, for the President does not have to announce in advance just how far Congress must move toward his views before he will sign the bill. This position is perfectly well understood in Congress; those members who desire to accomplish something, as opposed to just making a record of stances taken, have to take these facts constantly into account. Thus, a constitutive rule—the veto procedure—which on its face merely provides for a *last* stage in the legislative process, reaches all the way back to the beginning of that process, and most complexly influences the process from beginning to end. And, when the President and Congress are of different minds, the veto power can strongly affect the substance and quality of legislation, since substantial compromise is virtually forced on Congress, and a consistent and coherent policy is made nearly impossible.

But this, important as it is, may not exhaust the effect of the veto power, for that power would seem to have a clear tendency to facilitate expansion of Presidential powers in general. The situation is this: if the President, acting under a claim of inherent "executive" power, or under some other legal claim, does a certain thing, and if Congress seeks to disaffirm or to undo that thing, then the President can veto the congressional measure aimed at disaffirming his own action. For example, in "recognizing" Soviet Russia, President Franklin Roosevelt entered into an agreement accepting an assignment from the Soviet government of its own claims against funds held in the United States by former Czarist corporations. If Congress had disapproved of this step, and desired to annul it, veto of the annulling action would undoubtedly have occurred. Since veto in all cases of this form is absolutely certain, and since override is so small a probability, it is not unreasonable to conjecture that congressional acquiescence in presidential claims of power, now habitual in all but the extremest cases, is powerfully affected by the known existence of the veto, and the certainty of its use. It seems to me probable that this has been one of the principal causes of the continual accretion of power to the Presidency.

Let me give one final example, lightly referred to earlier. Gluckman draws on his own and others' work to make the point that the structure of society, by creating multiple and cross-cutting ties, may strongly support the stability of the society as a whole, and prevent it breaking asunder into parties utterly alien in interest and loyalty. There is much similar work to be done on the American Constitution, considered as it works more than as it reads.

Herbert Wechsler, the giant on whose shoulders stand all of us who try to see as far as we can into the deep structure of our Constitution, long ago did the classic analysis of the working of *political structure,* rather than rules of law judicially uttered, to maintain the influence and power of the States as such in our federal system.

Our Constitution appears to divide authority between the national government and the States, by enumerating the powers that are to belong to the nation, and by then explicitly reserving all other powers to the States. This division, in theory, could be policed by the judiciary, with the Supreme Court at the top, for that Court clearly has the power to declare an Act of Congress unconstitutional, on the ground of its entering an area outside the granted national powers. Indeed, this mode of policing has been tried. The trouble turned out to be that the granted national powers are so broad, and so strategically located, that Congress can find within them the means of dealing effectively with virtually any subject, and the Court has not found (and could not have found) any intellectually respectable or principled stopping-place. This simplifies, but correctly states the overwhelmingly dominant trend in our history. Thus, one must say that federalism, as a matter of sheer *law*, has failed; the national Congress can do pretty much what it wants to do, while not going beyond the powers granted it in the Constitution, as these powers have been interpreted by the Supreme Court.

Yet our States, as Wechsler saw, remain important entities, governing many concerns of real significance. Congress has been very far from using its powers, as they might have been used, to supersede State power in all matters. Wechsler located the solution to this puzzle in the *political structure* of the national government. From this point, for brevity, I paraphrase him very freely, intermixing some points of my own.

The Senate, of course, is destined by the law of its composition to be the guardian of the interest of the States as such, since two Senators come from each state, regardless of population, in a nation wherein State population varies in a ratio of something like 70:1. The most likely way at which State and national interest could collide would be the situation in which strong national desire contradicted the desires of people in the less populous states. The latter have an immense advantage in the Senate. This advantage goes further than the mere power to block; it generates power to force *affirmative* action, as the price of removing the block.

But, as Wechsler goes on to point out, the state legislatures have power over the House of Representatives for it is the legislatures who carve out, within each state, the districts from which Congressmen are sent. At the time Wechsler wrote, this power was larger than it is today, for considerable differences in the populations of different districts within a State were permitted; the Supreme Court now requires something close to exact population equality, and, by constitutional amendment, restrictions on the franchise—which meant, in practice, the prevention of black voting—are also outlawed. But the state legislatures still draw the Congressional district lines. In many states, moreover, the *number* of districts may change after a decennial national census, for such a census may, and often does, alter the number of Congressmen to which the state is entitled. In practice, this may mean that the state legislature will be deciding who is to be squeezed out. Even where this does not happen, the "equal population" formula that is now a requirement of law as to districts will often, in a multidistrict state, make a fairly substantial change in district lines necessary every ten years, since population within the state will often have shifted. Even with the requirement of equal populations, a very large (perhaps infinite) number of ways of carving up the state will be possible, and some of these will be more advantageous to incumbents than will others. It is the fact that, while redistricting is going on in the state legislature, many Congressmen are in close touch with the process; this concern must obviously lead them to maintain friendly relations with the state legislators.

The President, under the electoral college system, is elected on a state-by-state basis. The aim, in theory, is not to win as many votes as possible in Iowa, but to "carry" Iowa, in which case you get *all* the Iowa electoral votes. If Iowa were the only concern, then you would aim at carrying Iowa by the biggest possible overkill. But you are also trying to carry forty-nine other states, one by one, each as a separate entity, and your Iowa strategy must be influenced by this.

Most important of all, it seems to me, is a thing Wechsler does not, I believe, expressly touch on, as he was interested mainly in the purely constitutional structure, rather than in the structures of party and other political organizations that have developed within it. I refer to the necessity under which Congressmen, Senators, and Presidential candidates lie, of cooperating with the political people who are active in state politics. To take this on the party level, and to start with the Presidency, a Democratic candidate for President who wants to carry Iowa must cooperate with and rely on the Iowa Democratic leaders— usually people who at the very same time are interested in the Iowa state government. The strict state-by-state system on electoral votes makes this necessary cooperation a strict state-by-state matter. The very same thing is true of senatorial and congressional candidates. The Senator, running statewide, is under the imperative of keeping on good terms with the statewide leadership in his party, and this statewide leadership, in turn, is interested in the continuing importance of state government, for many people in state politics, though their support is important—often indeed crucial—to the candidate for federal office, have no aspirations beyond state politics. These same considerations, without going through them in detail, affect congressional candidates within their districts.

To all this it may be added that a good many Senators and Congressmen have a background of activity in state politics; this probably engenders a spirit of respect for state institutions and their problems. It is also true that one of the easiest ways by which Congress avoids a troublesome problem is to "leave it to the States"—and it is also true that Congress may often make a good-faith judgment that a certain area of concern may be better handled by the States. But the structures Wechsler explored undoubtedly give firmness to the continuingly successful claim of the States to ongoing existence and to ruling many important matters.

The Congressman, then, is in a classic situation of cross-cutting loyalties. His major accomplishments must be on the national level, and if he is to accomplish anything important he will in most cases have to get along reasonably well with the national leadership of his party in Congress. He is, on the other hand, totally dependent for survival on his constituency, which can and usually must, to some extent at least, be changed in contours by the state legislature, when it redistricts the state. Yet he cannot change it, though it can be altered either so as substantially to erode his power base, or else in a manner reflecting sympathy to him.

I have sampled some thoughts and work which seem to me to move toward what one might call a social anthropology of politics in a populous and powerful nation. I think the study of American politics would benefit from social anthropological work along the lines of Gluckman's studies in tribal constitutional law.

There seems to me to be one imperative requirement of such studies. They ought to focus on the largely self-knowing inner culture of "political" people, the people who hold or seek office, together with those who make either a life's work or a strong avocation of managing politics. This is a group with vague and easily passable boundaries; a rigorous "definition" would do more harm than good, because it might result in the overlooking or exclusion of something important. But it is not very hard, in most cases, to answer the question whether an individual is actively in politics, or is merely voting, or expressing occasional political interests within groups not primarily political. The array of real politicians is very small in number, in comparison with the whole population. Political people tend to know and to react to each other, or to have common connections. The constitutional framework structures their activity; it is structured also by party organization. The interesting thing to look at would be the dynamics within these structures, the sometimes far-reaching *reactions* to constitutional channelings.

Such a line of work would not exclude consideration of mass sentiments and desires, or of anything else concerning the whole people. These things are what politicians work with and upon; this is the raw material of their art, and that art, with all its patternings, cannot be understood without keeping this fact in mind. But no clarity about the structures of politics can be attained until one separates out from the mass those people whose activities constitute and form political structure.

It is this very separating out of the political people, it seems to me, that makes anthropological study of politics a possibility. An "anthropology" of public opinion or of the patterns of mass voting might be encompassed by the etymology of the word, but has little to do with the insights and methods of such anthropological work as has actually been done. On the other hand, an anthropological study, for example, of the United States House of Representatives is not only a clear possibility, but would benefit greatly from the very insights of Gluckman, and of the tradition he lived in and so adorned.

THE THIRD CENTURY OF THE
AMERICAN REPUBLIC*

When it was about this time of day here at The Hague, on July 4, 1776, it was about noon in Philadelphia. Americans like to talk everything out, and the Continental Congress was after three days still locked in debate over the verbal details of an utterance already resolved upon. Hours later, while this town slept through a silent Dutch night of the eighteenth century, punctuated perhaps by time-telling bells or the night-watch's cry, the debate in Philadelphia, which had gone into the evening there, closed at last. A certain motion was put and carried, and a process of signing was begun and completed. When The Hague began to stir the next morning, with the sounds of walking, and vendors' voices in narrow streets, something new had come into the world.

That new nation is not yet very old. Since a good many people live past a hundred years, it is certain that a few now living were born before the last person died who had been born before the United States of America came into being. That is the age of our nation—two human lives, very long to be sure, but well within the range of normality. To put it another way, since the fathering of children by men past 60 is not even very unusual, it is nearly certain that the world of the living, right now, holds persons whose grandfathers were not only alive on July 4, 1776, but old enough to have read of the Declaration.

*Bicentennial Independence Day Address, delivered at The Hague, 4 July 1976, in the presence of Her Majesty Queen Juliana and the Prince Consort.

It is not the hour, yet, to judge at all of the place in history of the United States—any more than the year 1266 A.D. would have been a good year in which to sum up the meaning in history of the English kingdom reorganized and given a new start in 1066, by William the Conqueror.

The title I have given my speech tells its own story. You and I may be—indeed we must be—interested in history, the inexhaustible fountain of political wisdom, but we are concerned above all, for "ourselves and our Posterity," with the *next* American century. About that century, we can today only make forecasts based on trends we think discernible.

I have to give one early warning. In the first part of my talk, I shall speak of certain trends in American life which seem to me wholly good in themselves. In what comes later, I shall state what I believe to be the critical and as yet not adequately faced threat to all the good hopes we hold. Please keep this in mind as I speak; if you do not, the affirmative things I shall begin with may seem expressions of a nearly idiotic optimism, more suitable to a flag-waving rally than to an occasion calling for a "decent respect for the opinions of mankind." Before I am through, you will see that my vision of America is, in the touching phrase of Keats, one of trembling hope—realistic certainly in its trembling, realistic too, I think, in its hope.

I would begin by saying that my own being here on such an occasion and in such a role can tell you something important about the United States of America. I am a man who, insofar as he is known at all, must be known as being, in age as in youth, of a political persuasion fundamentally different from that of our President and most of those in his party. I do not mean by this that I am a Democrat rather than a Republican, although that is true. I mean that I am known, if at all, as someone who perceives political and above all economic justice quite differently from the manner in which these things are perceived among the prevalent party in our Executive Branch today. This fact is not hidden. Yet the persons in charge of these things—either knowing this or, as is far more likely and far more significant, not even thinking to look into the matter—have warmly invited me to address you on this great day, in some sense on behalf of the United States of America, though saying exactly what I as a private citizen see fit to say.

This fact, as a single fact, speaks for itself. Nor is the widest suggestion it can convey a false one. We Americans have up to this point, within human limits and with some bad passages, made good on our promise of freedom of expression—both of expression explicitly political and of expression only implicitly political, if it is political at all—freedom of opinion and freedom in way of life. There can never be enough freedom, as there can never be enough charity, but we can truthfully say not only that our freedom is in health but, even more importantly, that it seems to be growing healthier all the time.

When I spoke to European audiences in the summer of 1970, one of our long, hot summers of student revolt and urban rioting, I was often asked the question, "Is the United States a *suppressive* country?" I always replied that, since all societies practice some degree of suppression, the answer to the question must be a relative one, and that the only way to establish a scale of measurement for this relative judgment must be to ask, "What country, in the history of the world, has ever endured so much and so bitterly expressed dissent with as little suppressive re-action as we have seen in the United States in the last two years?" No questioner ever attempted an answer. There is no such coun-try. Some suppression there was, and some tragic incidents in no way excusable. But in overwhelming part, we kept to the path of moderation and tolerance.

We have moved now into quieter waters. And in these latest years has come, I think, an even steadier spirit of acceptance—easy and habitual acceptance—not only for political opinions but, as I have said, for ways of life. Taboos of all sorts—the old and cruelly irrational taboos of a parochial frontier—have been and are falling. Such trivial and vital things as (for one example

of each) the length of one's hair and the practice of family plan-
ning, were in my own youth subject to constricting pressures in
large parts of society. Today—with those exceptions which always have to be allowed for in the real world—freedom as to
these and thousands of other such matters is simply taken for
granted.

I am speaking today principally of our third century, and of
course I cannot know whether this now strong and clearly visible trend of continuing liberation will go on. But on every
reckoning of probability it seems likely that it will. No omi-
nously threatening counterpressures are felt. That is the most
any country can say of any of its desires and yearnings for times
to come.

In this sense, then, we have kept our promise to the world.
We unfurled the flag of liberty, and that flag is flying more
proudly today than ever before. It shows no signs of drooping.

Freedom was our promise in 1776, but black slavery was
our heritage. What can I tell you of our painful progress toward
racial justice? A great part of my own life's work as lawyer and
writer has gone into this effort, and I know whereof I speak. It
would be, quite simply, a lie for me to say to you that all is well.
But I can honestly say to you that the progress that has been
made, particularly in our South, has been stupefying, quite outside the limits of the rationally expectable.

The Austin, Texas of my boyhood was a beautiful and highly
civilized Southern city. But you never saw a black in any other
than a menial occupation. Black intellectuals there were, but
they kept to themselves, for their very existence was looked on
as a mixture of a joke and an affront. Black people went to the
back doors of white people's houses. It was obligatory that they
be called by their first names. Segregation was absolute, from
the maternity ward to the cemetery. Black people moved with
docility to sit in the back of the trolley-car, in a special section
reserved for them—in this and in hundreds of other ways being
forced to act out through every day a charade betokening their

unfitness to be part of the general life of the community. Their political power was zero. No black was ever found on a jury, though many sat in the prisoner's seat. Lynching did sometimes occur, and was always there in the background; I well remember that one had to be careful in expressing one's disapproval of lynching, for lynching was seen, rightly, as the indispensable ultimate weapon of a frankly and wholly racist regime.

A couple of years ago, I happened to be describing these bad old times to a group of young people, black and white, in a public place in Austin, my old home. As I spoke, I noticed they were growing restless, and were exchanging puzzled looks. Suddenly I realized why. They didn't believe me. They thought I was putting them on. And I laughed inwardly, not in amusement but in the triumph of a footsoldier in a victorious army, whose enemy has been so obliterated that its very existence is not believed in.

Of course the picture is not everywhere as good as that. But the trend is steeply upward, and there is no reason to think it will be reversed.

To have made a promise of freedom two hundred years ago, and to stand today in an era of continually expanding freedom— to have started with one of the worst systems of slavery in history, and to stand today where one can hardly see the unvenerated ruins of the old unashamedly racist system—these achievements would in themselves be, and are, grounds for hope, even if we had not meanwhile found time and strength for such enterprises as coming with the help that was needed, even by people of your sacrificial courage, to combat with you the obscenity of Hitler—now also nearly unbelievable.

Why, then, is the hope a trembling hope? The answer is applicable alike to our pride in freedom and to our pride in our progress against racism. The answer is poverty. As freedom has opened road after road, poverty has continued so to hobble many of us that the beckoning roads cannot be trod. As the overt humiliations of racism have begun and so largely completed their exit, black people remain, on the whole, poorer than others, very many of them too poor to walk through any of the doors that have opened.

I think you know that I am not talking about a poverty comparable, say, to that found in parts of Africa. Total destitution is rare in America, as it is, of course, with you. We are not dealing with mass starvation. But far, far too many of our people—disgracefully many in so rich a nation—are living at a level of subsistence which makes largely irrelevant, to them, the existence of a freedom and an equality they have not the means to enjoy.

The "American Dilemma" used to be found in the fact of overt and raw racism confronting the abiding presence of an ideal of equality. Our dilemma now is the contradiction between that same abiding ideal and the fact of a poverty which, at its worst, makes mockery of all formal equality and all formal freedom.

We may hope then, but we must hope in anxiety. Our task is plain. We must return for inspiration to our beginning, and realize that the philosophers of our Revolution, following after John Locke, were right when they saw *property* as of an importance making it suitable to be mentioned along with liberty—if by "property" we mean a secure enjoyment of the means of a decent material life. The possession of property, so defined, is indispensable to the enjoyment of every kind of equality, and of all liberty—indispensable to "the pursuit of happiness." We will live in a state of quite unacceptable self-contradiction until we begin, at least, to address this master-problem with a suitable seriousness, and with the resolve to go on, decade after decade, until the task is accomplished.

So that is how we start our third century—with freedom much grown and still growing, with our old devil of overt racism nearly exorcised, but with the unfulfilled obligation so to restructure our dealings with the material base of life as to make these blessings valuable to all of us. After such accomplishments, who could not have hope? In the face of such a task, who would not tremble?

I have said nothing so far about our recent turmoils around the Presidency. Such catastrophes of character can happen to any nation; in our case, we took care of the matter, in pain but on the whole with dignity. I think we came out of the experience a little wiser, a little more aware of the infinite possibilities, for lowness as well as for nobility, in human nature. I have said nothing yet about the agonizing war in Viet Nam; whatever may be the final word of history on that war, it now seems to almost all of us to have been a bleak national wrong, into which we all but sleepwalked. I think we have waked. I think we have firmly learned, among other things, two important truths—that we as well as others are capable of inexcusable wrong, and that the power of the United States, though it can and should remain— or, if you like, again become—a force for good in the world, is far from sufficient for controlling the whole world's destiny. We have learned what it means to lose, and to deserve to lose. We have fully grown up.

Above all, we have learned, out of these recent events, one thing of an importance transcending all other lessons. We have at last located the enemy. Catherine the Great was much disturbed by the Declaration of Independence, and would have brought about our defeat if she could have done so. Hitler detested us and all our ideals and goals. In these people across the sea, and in many others, we have thought to have located the enemy. Now we know better—infinitely better. We have learned, as all peoples must if they are not to be lost, that the wiliest, the most pertinacious enemy to all our hopes and to all our dreams is ourselves. That is a bitter lesson, but no one even so much as guesses what wisdom may be until that bitter lesson is learned.

Out of these experiences, and above all out of this insight, has come a great national sorrow. The most important and the most heartening thing about our third century is just that sorrow. If I could stand here today and tell you that we have no sorrow about the past, and no anxiety about the future, then you would have to conclude that there was no hope for us, that our moral force had been quite spent in our first two centuries. But what I have to tell you is that we are a people in sorrow, and that we face our third century with anxiety. And therefore hope is possible. Hope is born of sorrow. Not surprisingly, this thought came to me, for utterance on this occasion, on last Easter Day, but the truth of Easter is perennial and eternal, and manifests itself in all things.

We are then sorrowful, and so we can be filled with hope. Our country contains thousands, indeed millions of people— in politics and elsewhere—who feel this sorrow, and so are will- ing to work and to give toward the fulfilment of this hope. Their proportion amongst us is probably at least as great as the pro- portion, in 1776, of dedicated believers in the doctrines of the Declaration of Independence.

I will not then say that I have *faith* that our third century will move us much closer to the working of our ideals into life. The object of faith ought not to be anything of human making— not even a nation. Faith is not faith if it can be disappointed by anything that happens. I will say rather that I have *hope*—hope solidly rooted, as hope must be among humankind, in sorrow.

We are sometimes apologetic about our national anthem— partly because it is rather hard to sing, but mostly because overt patriotism embarrasses us. I have never partaken of this feeling. Our national anthem is a noble poem that tells of a flag that stayed in place through darkness and doubtful battle—a symbol, surely, possessing beauty and power. "The rockets' red glare, the bombs bursting in air, gave us proof *through the night* that our flag was still there." We have lately, as many times in the remoter past, been through darkness and doubtful battle. But the very battle has lit up the flag. We are a people who could go to war in Viet Nam—but we are also a people who could first tolerate and then in overwhelming numbers join a protest against that war which forced its abandonment. We are a people who could make a fearful mistake in our choice of a President—but we are a people who could at last close ranks, without regard to party, to demand and in the end virtually to compel the departure from office of the person mistakenly chosen. Earlier on, we were a people who could practice a raw and undisguised racism—but we were a people among whom protest against that racism never died, but grew and grew, until at last the old inveterate evil limps mortally wounded. Through all darkness, there has been enough light, arising out of the very clash of battle, for us to see that our flag was still there.

There will be other darkness, other battles, in our third century. Nor can we anticipate that, at the end of that century, equality and freedom will have been unproblematically blended and reconciled, and that every one of us will be secure in the indispensable material base—the *property* base—to the enjoyment of these. But we can hope, on the solid ground of experience and even with good cheer, that our battles, even if not easily or entirely won, will not have been wholly lost, and that our flag will still be there.

In this hour, then—the two hundredth anniversary of those last long moments of anxious debate in Philadelphia—I speak to you my own belief that, when The Hague—the seat of government of one of our most steadfast friends among nations—wakes tomorrow morning to greet the third American century, that century should be and will be seen as one in which our country, richer in dearly bought self-knowledge, chastened by sorrow, can still worthily carry its part of the hope of earth.

EPILOGUE (16 September 1985):

It must be evident that, for a person who could deliver the above address, and in particular its last paragraph, the nine years since the delivery have brought much troubling change, in regard to the very matters touched upon in the address itself. But the above text foretold "other darkness, other battles. . . ." I cannot let these dark times destroy my hope for the American Republic. I am reminded of a line of poetry:

"They worked . . . and work is a kind of hope."

Let us hope, by the act of working for it, that the American Republic may soon resume its quest after its own soul. Less than a tenth of the "Third Century" is gone; it is too early for despair—if indeed there ever is a right time for despair.—C.B.

NATIONAL LAWMAKING
BY INITIATIVE?
LET'S THINK TWICE*

Second Lieutenant Napoleon Bonaparte, still in his teens, was back home in Corsica, on leave from his regiment, while our Philadelphia Constitutional Convention was meeting. Beethoven, about the same age as Napoleon, was teaching music to the children of his patroness. The steam engine was not yet at all practical. Poland was between her first and second partitions; Catherine the Great was on the throne of All the Russias. The man who discovered that lightning was electrical had come as a delegate to the Convention itself. But electrical technology was marching on. Volta was soon to devise an electrical battery that worked fairly well, though it would be 33 years before the magnetic effect of electric current would be discovered by Oersted. About 70 years were still to pass before Japan emerged from isolation, and before the publication of *The Origin of Species.*

The changes have been of such sort that it is doubtless impossible for us to imagine how the world looked and felt to those people in Philadelphia. Yet—while Poland was 120 years partitioned, then re-emerged as a nation, while our own great railroad system was building and declining, while Japan was defeating China and Russia, while the Hohenzollern emperors came and went, while Hitler triumphed and fell, while power dwarfing steam put humans on the moon—the Constitution

*Address to Biennial Conference, American Civil Liberties Union, 1979. Originally published in the Fall 1979 issue of *Human Rights,* a publication of the American Bar Association Press.

those people devised, in about a hundred days in Philadelphia, has stood without important change in its essential constitutive features, right down to now, and has grounded and channeled at least as much stability and desirable progress as any constitution in the history of the world. Reverence in the full sense may be inappropriate for the work of humans, but fear and trembling are just the right emotions for approaching a major change in the essential constitutive structure of a plan with such a history.

By "essential constitutive structure" I mean the ways of constructing the organs of government that are to have authority, of defining their power relations with one another, and of setting the procedures by which they make and execute law—and therefore policy. This material is the heart of any constitution; all else, however valuable it may be, is not of the constitutive essence.

Most of the amendments to our Constitution have not touched this essential structure at all. The 12th, 20th, 22nd and 25th Amendments made minor changes in the rules of eligibility and choice for the Presidency. These changes were perhaps not all to the good; the 25th Amendment has so far had only the result that Richard Nixon, already badly discredited and clearly on his way out, got to appoint his own successor. (It might be wise to ponder that illustration before sitting down again with paper and pencil and trying to think up something that might possibly work a little better than what we have.) But none of these amendments was of strategic importance.

The same may be said, I think, of the 17th Amendment, providing for popular election of Senators, instead of their election by the state legislatures. The ultimate constituencies remained the same—the states, one by one—and the reality was already in many places different from the form; who remembers that the 1858 Lincoln-Douglas Debates were between two candidates for the Senate who had to be elected formally by people other than the people whom they were addressing?

For nearly 200 years, then, the power structure of the American Constitution has remained just about the same. That will no longer be true if a constitutional amendment is adopted providing for an "initiative" mode of passing laws.

As I read the recent literature on this subject, I have to wonder whether people realize how deeply invasive and hazardous this surgery would be. The metaphor is exact. Such surgery should be consented to only in case of near-desperation; no competent doctor would perform comparably drastic surgery on the ground that it might do a little good to a patient not very sick.

The essence of the "initiative" amendment introduced by Senators Abourezk and Hatfield provides, simply, for the enactment of laws by majority vote of those people voting on the proposed law, in a national election.[1] That is the heart of the

---

1. The Abourezk and Hatfield proposal for national lawmaking by initiative, Senate Joint Resolution 67, 95th Cong., 1st Session, 123 CONG. REC. §11584:

> "*Resolved by the Senate and House of Representatives of the United States of America in Congress assembled,* (two-thirds of each House concurring therein) That the following article is proposed as an amendment to the Constitution of the United States, which shall be valid to all intents and purposes as part of the Constitution if ratified by the legislatures of three-fourths of the several States:
>
> "ARTICLE _____
>
> "Section 1. The people of the United States shall have the power to propose and enact laws in accordance with this article, except with respect to carrying out the powers granted to Congress in clauses eleven and fifteen of article I, section eight, of this Constitution. This article does not grant the people of the United States the power to propose amendments to this Constitution.
>
> "Section 2. A law is proposed by presenting to the chief law enforcement officer of the United States a petition that sets forth the text of the proposed law and contains signatures, collected within the eighteen months prior to such presentation, of registered voters equal in number to 3 percent of the ballots cast in the last general election for President and which includes the signatures of registered voters in each of ten States equal in number to 3 percent of the ballots cast in the last general election for President in each of the ten states. Within ninety days of such presentation, the chief law enforcement officer of the United States shall determine the validity of the signatures contained in such petition through consultation with the appropriate States. Upon a determination that such petition contains the required number of valid signatures, he shall certify such petition.

matter. I will discuss this main point, and comment later on some very important matters of procedure.

There is no way of knowing how much use would be made of this new lawmaking procedure, and there is no use trying to guess for an indefinitely long future—or even for the near future. The proposed "initiative" must, therefore, be treated simply as an alternative, that is, to Congress and the President, in their mandated coaction, as it has been since 1789.

Now I haven't read a great deal of the literature supporting this scheme. But I am surprised that I could have started to read any single piece of that literature without finding it said, not more than 10 lines from the beginning, that the most easily visible effect of this "initiative" plan would be the affording of a complete bypass to the Senate of the United States. The House of Representatives is constituted roughly on a population basis, roughly, then, a law that could pass the nationwide plebiscite might be expected to pass the House. For reasons that will appear, I think this to be a prediction only very roughly sustainable, but let it stand for now. The point now is that in the Senate the states are represented equally, without regard to their populations.

He shall then direct that the proposed law be placed on the ballot at the next general election hall for choosing Members of the House of Representatives occurring at least one hundred and twenty days after such certification. The Congress shall provide by law reasonable procedures for the preparation and transmittal of such petitions. For the purposes of this section, the term 'State' shall include the District of Columbia.

"Section 3. A proposed law shall be enacted upon approval by a majority of the people casting votes with respect to such proposed law and shall take effect thirty days after such approval except as otherwise provided in the proposed law. Any law enacted pursuant to this article shall be a law the same as any other law of the United States, except that any law to repeal or amend a law enacted pursuant to this article during the two years immediately following its effective date must receive an affirmative roll-call vote of two-thirds of the members of each House duly elected and sworn. No law, the enactment of which is forbidden the Congress by this Constitution or any amendment thereof, may be enacted by the people under this article.

"Section 4. The Congress and the people shall have the power to enforce this article by appropriate legislation."

Over half the American people live in 9 states, with 18 Senators. The highest population ratio between any 2 states is over 65:1. Thirteen states together have less than half the population of California or of New York; Texas alone is more populous by a good deal than these same 13 states. Close to half the American people live in the 14 New England, Middle Atlantic and East North Central states. You can put all this in many ways, but it all comes down to one thing: national popular-vote initiatives could easily succeed with respect to laws—any number of laws—that would have no chance whatever of passage in the Senate.

Nor can it be believed that this would be just a random matter. The initiative procedure would obviously call out to and attract any group that anticipated defeat in the Senate. Unless politics is entirely without logic or even sense, it must be expected that this procedure would become an established way to get around the Senate.

You may not like the senatorial system, but it was the price of union, an indispensable part of the Great Compromise of 1787. It is hard to believe that the expansion of this country over so vast a territory was not facilitated by it. It is not all clear that it is not of great benefit even today, as one of the political safeguards of the federalism we have considered one of our chief sources of political strength. Are we really willing to throw it up? Well, I think that question should be talked about a little more than it has been. If this proposal shows signs of life and growth, I much hope that many senators will themselves consider whether their own responsibility, to their states as states, can consist with a vote for this plan. A senator from Wyoming or Vermont, or even from Utah or Rhode Island, might want to calculate how many square blocks in Chicago it would take to out-vote the whole people of one of those states in a nationwide referendum.

I know I am talking to people who must believe in the spirit as well as the most literal letter of the Constitution, and I take leave therefore to doubt whether this plan is constitutional, even as an amendment. The amending article of the Constitution, Article V, provides that no amendment shall ever be passed that deprives a state of its equal representation in the Senate. Now the *effective value* of this guarantee derives entirely from its giving each state an equal voice in a Senate empowered as a law-making—and, of course, most importantly, a law-refusing—body. I wonder if, consistent with the spirit and obvious purpose of this provision for continued equal representation in the Senate, we can lawfully put in force, even by constitutional amendment, a plan that short-circuits the Senate altogether, whenever that seems desirable. If the freedom of speech should be taken to mean the freedom to speak in ways and in places that make possible *effectiveness* of the speech, then perhaps the guaranteed equal representation in the Senate should be taken to mean "equal representation in a Senate having *effectively* those powers which made the promise of equal representation a thing of value." Would you think that guarantee honored if each state could send two Senators to a Senate reduced to the function of rendering advisory opinions only, without power to act bindingly? But the "initiative" proposal will reduce the Senate to powerlessness, and strip the less populous states of the protection of the senatorial system, each and every time it works. This line of thought ought to be carefully considered by congressmen and senators; a vote for this initiative proposal may be a vote inconsistent at least with the spirit of the Constitution, as well as being, in many cases, a vote against the legitimate interests of their own states.

Let's go on to the presidential veto. That, too, is not to play a part in the "initiative" plan. Are we ready for that as well? Strangely, I haven't seen the question written about. Wilson, in his *Congressional Government,* spoke of this veto power as incomparably the greatest of the presidential powers. If you read Article II, you may decide that it is very nearly the only one the President has that does not rest on acquiescence by Congress.

There can be little doubt that bypassing the veto would enormously weaken the presidency, with incalculable consequences as to the possibility of presidential leadership, in regard to legislative programs especially, but in regard to other matters as well. In the world of today, are we ready to take that chance?

No senatorial system, no presidential veto. Well, those are two rather big masses of tissue to take out of the body of a patient who seems pretty healthy, all in all. It is not too much to say that this initiative proposal repeals, to an extent not now to be foretold, those parts of the Constitution that bestow the lawmaking power.

But I don't think the problems stop there. Probably more important than either of the two things just discussed is the lack, in this initiative proposal (or in any I can imagine), of provision for any responsible *deliberation,* by people elected for the purpose of deliberating.

The proposal provides that signatures may be collected, for up to 18 months before presentation to the Attorney General, on a petition *already containing the text* of the proposed law. The Attorney General then has 90 days to verify the millions of signatures required. He then places the law on the ballot at the next congressional election.

I am sure minor variations on all this are possible, but they can't much change the general picture, which is:

First, the text of the law is finally fixed by the sponsors, before signature collection begins.

Secondly, no amendment at all is thenceforward possible. (How could this be changed? The signatures must all relate to the same law.)

Thirdly, as much time as nearly four years could pass before the vote is taken on this meanwhile unalterable text. (Eighteen months plus ninety days plus the interval between congressional elections. If this is the maximum time, perhaps a year and a half or two years would be a good guess for an average.)

Fourthly, many months after commitment to a draft that is both first and final, everybody votes, yes or no.

You know, I have quite a problem understanding how anybody can think that would be a good way to make national law.
In Congress, lawmaking normally proceeds by a genuinely de-
liberative process. Referral to committee is referral to a group
of specialists, assisted by staff. The committee process is one of
give-and-take, of perception and tackling of problems as to substance and as to wording—the process, in other words, by which
sensible people try to reach a sensible result in a binding enactment. Of course, this process does not always work at its
ideal best; continual improvement must be sought. But the now
proposed alternative contains not so much as a possibility of
anything of the sort—unless, of course, some unmandated and
unofficial process of prior deliberation is gone through, voluntarily in the particular case, by people neither elected nor
officially appointed. Would it further democratic ideals to have
this sort of deliberation done by people who are not elected, or
in any way publicly responsible, rather than by people who are
elected, and want to be re-elected? Even so, the enormous interval must remain between the start of signature collection and
the final vote, with no possibility of change to meet new
thoughts or new circumstances. I have myself participated, on
the fringes, in changes for the better, even after a bill reached
the floor.

In the loss of deliberation, one would also lose the possibility of compromise—sometimes the compromise necessary to
procure passage, and sometimes, even more significantly and
benignly, the kind of compromise that, without paying any great
price as to a bill's main goals, can increase its prospects of effectiveness by increasing the breadth of its acceptance. It seems
inevitable that a process that begins with an unalterable text and
ends, many months or even years later, with a vote of that text
up or down, will produce and even compel total polarization of
conviction and of argument.

There is another most significant and healthy kind of compromise that goes on continually, with respect both to the
House and to the Senate—compromise as to the person and

program of the elected representative. Groups may be induced to vote for someone with some of whose views they disagree, because on the whole that person is satisfactory to them. We lawyers tend, I think, to look on the Bill of Rights and the 14th Amendment as the chief safeguards of minority interests. I have given too much of my life to trying to do what I could to keep these constitutional guarantees going to disparage them, and I feel no impulse to do so. But I would also hate to have to do without the structural and procedural safeguards built into the essence of representative government. Let's stop a minute and remember that it is in the very definition of unpopularity that unpopular groups and causes will normally lose referenda; I think they are very likely to get a good deal more dignity and protection by being, sometimes, the last five percent needed to make up the crucial fifty-one.

Now let me change the subject and consider some of the things that would be opened to plebiscitic control by this "initiative" proposal. The version of the proposal I have been given seems to open up to "initiative" all matters that can be dealt with by national law, except the declaration of war, the calling out of the militia, and the proposal of constitutional amendments. Of course there may be other variations on this, but let's consider this one proposal.

Fiscal policy—taxing, borrowing and spending—are then to be malleable to this initiative procedure, as would the regulation of interstate and foreign commerce, and all aspects of the regime for aliens. The patent system could be abolished, or vastly strengthened; the construction of three super aircraft carriers could be mandated. Anything at all could be passed with regard to the District of Columbia.

And so on up and down through Article I, Section 8.

A reflective reading of that Section alone suggests yet another thing wrong with this proposal: it leads to and supports no *system* or *plan* of government. In Congress, a great deal is known and considered, especially in the responsible commit-

tees, about the interactions and interrelations of particular provisions. Such knowledge and consideration at least makes
possible, if it does not always produce, legislation that works
well within the general frame. Such knowledge and consideration would, by the "initiative" proposal, be made impossible
on the part of the people finally deciding, and a very likely, or
at least an invited, result would be a series of *ad hoc* interventions either ineffective or wreaking needless havoc.

But we have to go out from Article I, Section 8, because
congressional lawmaking powers are found throughout the
Constitution. I will mention only one—of great interest to me,
and I should think to you—the Article III congressional powers
to deal with the jurisdiction of the Supreme Court. Now if you
want to rest in the comfort of thinking that Article III passages
giving these powers over the courts really mean a whole lot less
than they seem to say, well and good. I do not think that to be
so, and I think that the judgment that it is so cannot be made
to stick, in a showdown. Just in case I am right, do you think
well of a scheme that would subject powers over the jurisdiction
of the federal courts to the hazard of agitation for some three
million signatures, followed by a plebiscite?

This proposal, as a whole, is a proposal for the unlimited
accommodation of single-issue politics, at the ultimate voting
level. It casts aside nearly every safeguard we have—the safeguard of the Senate, the safeguard of the qualified presidential
veto, the safeguard of mature and informed deliberation in both
houses of Congress, the safeguard of those softening compro-
mises that take place in most if not all instances of the choice
of a representative. It encourages simplistic solutions to problems piecemeal—a recipe for chaos. It could, by the way, easily
produce 50 or 100 proposals on every biennial ballot.

It is no inconsiderable objection, moreover, that this proposal would just about maximize the power of money in politics.
Money could, I think, get pretty much any proposal on the
ballot, as long as there wasn't a picture of Hitler right on the

petition. Maybe even then. You need the signatures of three percent of the voters, and money could find the three percent that wanted to sign. Money would have an immense advantage, too, in putting the affirmative case forward, through all the so-called media, toward election day, the day of the plebiscite. Of course, some impecunious causes might win through, but our recognition of the power of money is shown by the fact that you and I know that the first step the sponsors of such causes would have to take would be to try to raise money—and sometimes they could raise enough, and sometimes they couldn't. But money doesn't have to raise money; money can just go to work without fuss, collecting signatures from the people the computer prints out as good prospects, and putting a keen advertising firm on retainer.

Now I haven't said all I could about this "initiative" scheme, but I guess I've said enough to enable you to guess where I stand on it. I hope at least I have said enough to convince you that it is major surgery, drastically changing the power allocations and processes of the American government—unless we rely, I think it not too much to say fatuously, on its not being used very often. I hope I have convinced you, also, that it entails great risks. Why in the world, then, would we want to put it into effect—in all likelihood irreversibly, because its repeal, by a second constitutional amendment, would be virtually impossible?

The main arguments seem to be that the people somehow distrust government, and would feel greater participation if they could vote on laws directly, and that it is an "elitist myth" to think that wise lawmaking is not expectable from the plebiscitic process I have described.

I will meet the second of these arguments head on. I think it is an insult to the intelligence of the American people to flatter them with the suggestion that politics, lawmaking, and national policy formation do not call for expertness, professionalism, and the commitment of full time. These jobs are as complicated as law or medicine. They require committed professionals, as Lincoln was a professional, and Jefferson, John Quincy Adams, both Roosevelts, Truman, and all the best of our congressmen and senators. The case for specialization in politics is overwhelming.

But, to go back to the first point, the point most often made in support of the "initiative" proposal, the need for specialists does not contradict the need for participation by the people. The people under the present system have to judge records, positions and character, and they have to make their wants and beliefs known. I confidently assert that the system we have affords ample scope for these crucial judgments of positions, records and character, and ample opportunity to make these beliefs and wants known. Sometimes you don't get what you want, even when you make your wants known, because more people want something else, or because the representative honestly thinks you are wrong, or both. But that is both life and democracy; participation and winning must never be confused. Having participated a lot, I am well (if somewhat ruefully) aware of this truth.

Underneath it all, I think this initiative proposal is just another instance of our thinking that discontents and frustrations are referrable to the *form* of our government, that they are remediable by changing that form. I strongly urge you that our form of government is very, very far from being so defective as to justify major and risky surgery. The fault lies not in the form but in ourselves. Our representative democracy can and I daresay will respond to whatever energy, conviction and knowledge the American people can bring to choosing representatives and to presenting to those representatives their desires and thoughts. I hope we will not fiddle with the form, but will redouble and more directedly channel the energy, conviction and knowledge, the thoughts and the desires.

ON WORRYING ABOUT
THE CONSTITUTION*

I am not quite sure that my dear friend Betsy Levin has not been just a little worried about my title for this lecture—a sort of meta-worry, if I may use one of those fashionable phrasings that give an impression—without by any means guaranteeing the reality—of the user's supple command of the most up-to-date philosophical niceties. Perhaps some of you share this meta-worry; "Worrying About The Constitution" does seem a bizarre thing to be talking about on a serious occasion. I must meet this meta-worry head on.

The constitutive work of the American people, springing from a text put together in about a hundred days nearly two hundred years ago, counts four cardinal achievements:

First, there is the formation of a national government, adequately empowered for meeting national needs as these are perceived from time to time, while the smaller constituent entities—the States—are empowered to deal with all matters that for the time being are not perceived as requiring national action. This, I think, is something like a "$\pi = 3.1$" approximation to the American federal system as it actually stands and works. It is the way I would now describe American federalism to a foreign lawyer who wanted to be told the practical truth about it in a few words.

Secondly, there has been set in place a framework within

*The 1984 John R. Coen Lecture at the University of Colorado Law School. First published in the *University of Colorado Law Review,* Volume 55, Number 4, Summer 1984. Special thanks are due to Dean Betsy Levin of the University of Colorado Law School.

which the executive and the legislative powers at the center of this national government, both of them democratically based, can arrive at different balances between themselves from time to time, without—so far, at least—setting in motion an irreversible process leading to the final victory of one branch and the permanent eclipse of the other.

Thirdly, the American people have invented, and have given first to themselves and then to the world, the noble idea and, humanly speaking, the reality of a system of human rights that stands as a part of constitutional law, and thus, as a matter of law, binds all components of government.

Fourthly, there is the famous American institution of "judicial review," resting on the thought—clearly expressed in the constitutional text—that our Constitution is the sort of law that generates rules of decision for judges in their courts.

Now these are glorious achievements. Before they came into being, the world had not seen anything very much like them, though much of the world now admires and tries to imitate them. They have been the basis of the growth of a little country of some three million free citizens, living on or near the Atlantic coast of middle North America, to what our country is today.

Yet I think I am right in saying that many people do worry about them. In greatest part this worry is not so much about their practical usefulness as about their legitimacy, under that very Constitution whose essential working features they have become.

As we approach the bicentennial of 1787, I think it well that we ask ourselves the meta-worrisome question, whether we do well to worry quite so much.

I had hoped to deal systematically and severally with the commonest worries I hear expressed about each of these achievements—the merely perverse worry about the warrant in law for the exercise of judicial review, for which worry I think two aspirin and a good night's sleep are perhaps the best prescription; the quite different and very important worry about the compatibility of judicial review with the commitments of democracy; the worry about the legitimacy of our continuing to protect human rights not expressly named in the Constitution; the worry (for which I can proffer no very promising resolution) about the sliding of power, and in particular the power to initiate war, into the hands of the President; and the worry about the fact that the powers of the national government have become very broad. But though I will talk about any of these worries with any of you until I leave Boulder voluntarily or am ridden out of town on a rail, I have found myself forced to confine my talk tonight to the one I last mentioned—the worry about the broad and open-ended empowerments of the national government. I will say that this is at least a good place to begin, because the binary structure of our government at its political center, the functions of its judiciary, and the capacity of the nation to protect human rights, would all come to nothing if we did not have a real national government, adequately empowered to act as such.

Let us then turn to the first of the constitutional achievements of the American people—the achievement absolutely indispensable to the attainment of every other constitutional objective—the formation of a national government that may lawfully deal with all national needs. Worry about this sometimes takes a rather assertive and even accusatory tone, in something called "strict constructionism," but I am sure, from a lifetime of reading and listening, that many people who have not ritually embraced "strict constructionism," go about under the vague and rather saddening impression that there is something not quite according to Hoyle, something a little shady, about the variety and scope of present-day exercise of national power. Insofar as it has strength, this worry tends to the delegitimization of our national government as it stands and beyond any doubt will continue to stand. It is a feeling of baneful political value to those who want to be immune from effective control in the public interest.

I would make one special point here: In years to come, our national government will face new tasks, requiring new actions. To me, the chief of these tasks ought to be a radical redirection of theory and practice toward wiping out poverty in the United States. This is both a human rights problem and an empowerment problem. There is nothing but hypocrisy in our strutting and fretting about "human rights" on the stage of the world, while pussyfooting past the one human right without which all the others are sham—the right to a decent material basis for life. I hope that in talking about this we can stop talking "compassion" and start talking "justice," which it is the principal business of any government to establish. If we start moving this way, a great deal of the work will have to be done by Congress—just as Congress finally had to move massively against racism, even after the judiciary had lighted the path. The political difficulties will be very great; indeed, I would be discouraged now, if I didn't remember that I was already graying around the temples when the people who were supposed to know were telling us you never could get Congress to move against racism. I remember too—and this is the point I want principally to stress just now—that efforts to get Congress to move against racism were impeded by the suggestion of doubts—worries if you like—concerning Congress's *power* in the premises. These doubts—or worries—were of such stuff as dreams are made on; like dreams, they are hard now even to remember—though I shall partially refresh that memory a little later. But it would be a shame to go into the next great human rights battle, the fight against poverty, impeded by even the vaguest of worries as to the lawful power of this nation, as a whole nation, to do whatever it takes to establish this kind of justice, to secure the blessings of this kind of liberty, basic as it is to all other kinds. For this reason chiefly, there is seriousness of purpose, as well as reflective interest, in any attempt to deal with the vague worry that nags around the edges of our conceptions about national power.

I think this worry ought first to be addressed by pointing

out how broad a revisional enterprise it would be to confine the
United States government to enumerated powers, narrowly read.
We are not dealing with dubious expansion of one or two or
three clauses in the Constitution, or with recent departures
from a "strict construction" orthodoxy that prevailed from the
very beginning through those happy days just before the New
Deal. "Strict constructionists," unless they are perchance utterly
unprincipled, the mere manipulators of a slogan in service of
their present desires, would lay waste the government of the
United States as it exists, and repudiate most of our history as
tainted by illegitimacy. If we were to modify our national polity
to conform to narrow interpretive canons, we wouldn't need
any enemies; we would have destroyed ourselves. In this I intend
no hyperbole.

   This area of worry is often made to revolve around what is
now called (without definite warrant in the constitutional text)
the "interstate commerce" power. That is why, when I am about
to start a class down the familiar commerce-clause road, from
Gibbons v. Ogden[1] to *Wickard v. Filburn*[2] and beyond, I start off
with admiralty, then move on to patents—and then proceed to
some other national powers not much discussed in constitutional law courses. I draw the students' attention to the one and
only textual beginning for admiralty—an Article III grant of
judicial jurisdiction, to the *courts* of the United States, over "all
cases of admiralty and maritime jurisdiction." That is absolutely
all the Constitution has to say about admiralty. Yet the clause
has been held to adopt, by implication, a *substantive* maritime
law of national character, uniform throughout the country and
in some sense the world, and prevailing over state law; "maritime" tort law, for example, is even now expanding into new
areas. This admiralty clause has been held to confer on Congress
a power to enlarge (as well as to contract) the judicial jurisdiction early held to be comprised in the constitutional phrase, and

1. 22 U.S. (9 Wheat) 1 (1824).
2. 317 U.S. 111 (1942).

even to modify that substantive maritime law that had been held to be adopted by constitutional implication.

The patents and copyrights power has been construed with great liberality and even imagination. It serves the garment trade, among others, by what are called "design patents" on garment styles. Phonograph records and motion pictures are "writings" protectable by copyright—a broad analogic extension of the word "writings" that ought to be anathema to "strict constructionists."

Paper money issued by the United States is, by national law, legal tender for all debts public and private. That can hardly surprise you, if you read dollar bills. But try to find authority for it when you read the Constitution. The power to "raise and support armies" has radiated an enormous and complex network of national management. The power to establish post offices and post roads was long ago held to imply, among many other things, the power to punish by imprisonment the use of the mails to defraud. Congress has exercised enormous—virtually plenary—power over aliens and Indians; try to find *those* powers expressly given in the Constitution.

When we do turn, then, to the commerce power, I think my students have been brought correctly to view its expansive use as just another example of something that totally pervades the whole government, as to every power mentioned in or implied by the Constitution. It is the less surprising to them, then, that broad application of the commerce power starts very early. *Gibbons v. Ogden*[3] summarily settled two extremely important and by no means obvious points: first, that commerce includes navigation (which is, strictly speaking, only a *means* by which commerce, again in the strictest sense, is made possible) and, secondly, that the transportation of *human passengers* is commerce.

In *United States v. Coombs*,[4] decided in 1838 by a unanimous

3. 22 U.S. (9 Wheat) 1 (1824).
4. 37 U.S. (12 Pet.) 72 (1838).

Court with Justice Story writing, Coombs had been indicted
under a federal statute for stealing some goods that had been
brought ashore from a wrecked ship, "The Bristol" by name,
and left lying above high tide on Rockaway Beach on Long
Island. The Court based its upholding of the statute and the
indictment squarely on the commerce clause. My students, who
learned in childhood to lisp the phrase "interstate commerce,"
are not surprised when the first question I ask them about this
case is "Where had the ship Bristol been, and where was she
going?" Surprise does slowly dawn as they scan the entire report
and find that the nationality, provenience and destination of the
Bristol are nowhere mentioned. The Court didn't seem to care
about all that. Neither did the drafter of the indictment. Neither
did the draftsmen of the 1825 statute, which defines the crime
simply as stealing goods belonging to a wrecked ship, without
requiring, as an element of the crime, anything about the ter-
mini of the voyage. Is it any wonder that this case is conspicuous
for its absence, not only from modern casebooks and treatises
on constitutional law, but also from the supposedly comprehensive *Annotated Constitution of the United States?* It just doesn't
fit in with what we thought we knew. It would mix people up.

But even if we pass over this point, and assume *arguendo*
that the Bristol really was on a foreign or interstate voyage, and
that Congress, the United States Attorney who drew the indictment, Mr. Justice Story, and his brethren, all just forgot to
mention this as an element of the federal crime, the case has
real difficulties. These goods were lying on a beach in New York.
Stealing them was common-law or statutory larceny under New
York law. They might lately have been "in interstate commerce."
But now, at conjectural best, they were goods that used to be
"in interstate commerce." In the nature of the case, nothing is
known of their destination as of the time of larceny.

The 1871 case of *The Daniel Ball*,[5] unlike *Coombs*, has not

5. 77 U.S. (10 Wall.) 557 (1871).

simply flickered out of existence in the literature, but it is not often, I think, given the attention it deserves. One question in the case was whether certain federal safety regulations, designed to protect *passengers,* could be applied to a vessel that shuttled between two points in Michigan, but carried some *cargo* that was coming from or going to out-of-state points. (To the best of my knowledge, incidentally, it was in this case, decided eighty-four years after the Constitution was drafted, after the death not only of every Framer but of every Justice on the *Gibbons v. Ogden* and even the *United States v. Coombs* Court, that the word "interstate" achieved, in a Supreme Court opinion, its now conventional place as a gloss on "among the several States.") The *Daniel Bell* court upheld the application of the statute. Now you talk about pegs! The fact that some *cargo* was to be transhipped to go interstate was held to justify the imposition of regulations having to do with *passengers'* safety. Remember, these Justices were the real "old men of the tribe," the guardians of ancient ramparts, an ample generation closer to 1787 than they are to us.

One ought not to omit the Limitation of Shipowners' Liability Act of 1851. That Act, though now treated academically and in the practice as a part of admiralty law, was probably conceived of by the Congress that passed it as an exercise of the commerce power. The court upheld it, applied it quite regardless of any question about the sort of trade carried on by the vessel whose owner sought limitation, and applied it against very wide categories of claims, including personal injury. The underlying assumption (expressly stated in a Supreme Court opinion) had to be that drastic limitations of the recoveries of burned and crippled passengers, even where the ship was clearly at fault and liable, encouraged the investment of money in ships, and so promoted commerce. "Directly" or "indirectly"? The question is not answerable, because "directness" and "indirectness" are in the eye of the beholder-as-lexicographer. But this train of nineteenth century events, substantially completed before the Interstate Commerce Act of 1887 was passed, should clear away any illusion that genuine ancient ramparts were being manned by the Court that (for a relatively brief period) used this direct-indirect approach to strike down Acts of Congress regulating manufacture.

These older cases are in a continuous pattern with such more familiar and later cases as the *Shreveport Rate Cases*,[6] wherein that notorious subversive, Justice Hughes, wrote for a Court that upheld national dealing with certain completely internal railroad rates within Texas, on the ground of their effects on interstate shipment, and the Stockyard Case of 1922, wherein another Old Bolshevik, Chief Justice Taft, wrote for a Court that upheld detailed regulations of the local practices of stockyards, on the ground that these practices affected interstate movements of cattle.

In 1918, the year of *Hammer v. Dagenhart*,[7] wherein the Court struck down an Act of Congress prohibiting interstate shipment of goods made by child labor, Justice Holmes could say, in his dissent, that he had thought the point settled otherwise by the most conspicuous prior decisions of the Court, while the majority opinion could not cite a single case upholding its decision, but could only attempt to distinguish—on what seem to me (as to Holmes) constitutionally trivial grounds—cases that, broadly speaking, looked the other way. No ancient ramparts were being manned here. The ancient ramparts were and are imaginary.

Under the commerce power, then, just as under all the other powers—from taxation to patents, from spending to aliens—the United States has acquired, by a process never fully reversed, and but infrequently and then very little checked since our beginnings, a national government. If we look at this as a result or outcome, it is hard to see why anybody would worry about it or think it undesirable, since it means only that the nation as

6. Houston E. & W. Texas Ry. Co. v. United States, 234 U.S. 342 (1914).
7. 247 U.S. 251 (1918).

a nation *may* regulate any matter thought to need such regulation by the nation's political majorities in Congress—representatives of most of the people and Senators from most of the States—two very different things, as a glance at the constitutional arithmetic of the United States will show. And any proposed step must also have presidential approval, or else attain really staggering majorities in both Houses of Congress. But does this result, a genuine national government, however desirable it may be, deserve to have about it still the air of illegitimacy? Ought we still to worry about it?

Several very large factors form the background against which this question must in these late days be addressed. We can begin (and really might end) with the matter of authority. Who decided on the espousal of the creative, imaginative mode of interpretation that has, with as much consistency as is ever attained in large political affairs, marked the two-century life of the American Constitution? And did that decider, or those deciders, have the authority to decide on this interpretive course?

The answer to the first question is: *Everybody*—everybody who could be thought to have the power to make this decision. There is a persisting myth that places the Supreme Court, presided over first by the live and then by a ghostly John Marshall, in the role of lonely protagonist. But I think that view prevails for no better reason than that Supreme Court decisions are the easiest materials to find, and the handiest for using in casebooks. Beyond doubt John Marshall and his successors have played an important role in their reasoned discourse. But in every single case I have mentioned up to now, and in nearly all that I shall mention, and indeed in every one of the very large number of Supreme Court cases sustaining national authority, the Court has only been *validating* and *legitimating* some action already taken by Congress. Every claim to national authority thus validated in the Court, through our whole constitutional history, has already been espoused and decided on as right by the Senate, the House of Representatives, and the President—or, in rare

cases, by the two-thirds majorities in House and Senate required
to override a presidential veto. It is not just that these authorities are *en masse* quite impressive. It is that their enumeration
absolutely exhausts the possessors of national authority at the
top—the judicial, the legislative, and (except in the special case
of veto) the executive authority. There wasn't anybody else to
ask; Heaven is silent on this as on so many other practical questions. *The American People,* over two centuries, have had to decide not only on the policy of particular measures but also on
the constitutional legitimacy of modes of interpretation of the
Constitution. And they have decided, through all the representatives they have for dealing with national affairs, on those expansive modes that have in all their varieties made possible the
American government as we know it.

That in itself ought probably to settle the matter, and set
the worrying at rest. Speaking in the late eighteenth century on
a far more doubtful question, Blackstone said, as I recall, that
he need not and would not argue the legitimacy of the transfer
of power that took place in the Glorious Revolution of 1688,
because the question had been one not for his own generation
but for those he called "our ancestors." The principle he relied
on underlies all sound constitutionalism. And in our case it is
a principle of particularly mild and benign application, because
the most expansive interpretation of national powers does not
oblige Congress to use those powers in any way. If Congress
should come to desire it, and should persevere in a patient and
thorough work of demolition, the country could still be made
into that collection of fifty rustic and decaying-urban republics
dreamt of by "strict constructionists."

But there is another less categorically identifiable but no less
certain kind of acceptation that has been given to the broad
interpretive modes of American constitutional law. I get at it
with my students by telling them that there is not and for a very
long time has not been any principled constituency whatever for
anything within miles of "strict constructionism." I am referring

to the plain fact that there is as good as no group in the United States that does not want and indeed press for the exercise, in behalf of its *own* interests, of federal powers that cannot be dreamt to exist except by employment of the expansive modes of interpretation that are now habitual. You can read about this every day. A high official of the drug manufacturing company involved in a poisoning scare of yesteryear was quoted as saying that his firm was above all insistent on a *nationwide* set of packaging regulations, pre-empting all state and local authority; he didn't seem to have heard that murder by poison is a local crime, facilitated perhaps, but only "indirectly," by the want of protective packaging. In about the same edition of the *New York Times,* it was reported that bankers were pressing for a uniform national law overruling state laws that had invalidated the due-on-sale clause in real-property mortgages. Now there's a "local subject" for you! A little later we heard that the truckers, to serve us better, had won a national law forcing the States to allow on their highways truck-rigs of a size some States considered unsafe. The person who grieves over the constitutional impropriety of financing medical care on a national basis is not very likely to be someone who thinks the national government has no business dealing with narcotics or kidnapping. There is hardly anybody with any interest at all in the problem of resident aliens who wants Congress to abstain from regulating this subject, though some may desire primarily the tough comprehensiveness of a federal regime, while some may be more interested in the pre-emptive force of federal law, as against patchy and locally motivated state regulations.

The danger in listing examples is that the list may be thought exhaustive. The very contrary is true here; the desired uses of the national power, expansively construed, are practically infinite in number; the satisfaction of these desires saturates the national government.

It is important to bring up and so to emphasize that the American people's acceptance, through their lawful representatives and in the less formal ways just alluded to, of the expansive and creative modes of interpretation of national powers, is not a thing of yesterday or of the last few decades. As soon as the country began its existence under the present Constitution, the long war began. Probably the chief controversy just then was over the Bank of the United States, with Hamilton and Jefferson in the lead of the respective parties. The protective use of the tariff soon claimed eager attention. The use of federal funds for "internal improvements"—roads, bridges and canals— was bitterly protested against. Extensions of the admiralty power were assailed in the strongest possible language. The power of Congress to make paper money legal tender was first actually denied, and then affirmed, by the Supreme Court, not long after the Civil War. The 1904 decision in *Champion v. Ames*,[8] sustaining Congress in its prohibition of the interstate shipment of lottery tickets, was not a mere unnoted inadvertence; it drew four dissents, and was deplored by some as marking the demise of federalism. I think many people forget that the general question of expansive interpretation of national powers has been fought over and over and over again, with the result (reached, I remind you, by every authority that could conceivably be thought competent) always the same, in the not very long run. I doubt that any large and complex constitutional question in the history of the world has received as much consideration as this one, or been so clearly settled so many times.

Yet the new case, which usually ought to be treated as nothing but a footnote illustration of principles too well settled to be worth many words, is sometimes talked about as though it were a case of first impression, an impudent improvising of interpretative techniques hitherto unknown. One of the best modern illustrations is to be found in the discourse surrounding the passage and validation of the Public Accommodations Title of the Civil Rights Act of 1964. Fearing with good reason that the

8. 188 U.S. 321 (1903).

Court might fall back to old-fashioned views of "state action," which would have excluded the Fourteenth Amendment from application, Congress chose to base this Title mainly on the commerce clause, prohibiting racial discrimination in service by establishments that offered to serve interstate travellers, or that received a substantial proportion of their food by interstate shipment. In an ideal world, one might have preferred, for esthetic reasons, to rely on the Fourteenth Amendment, but the managers of the bill concluded that the prudent course was to rely on what they very naturally took to be an absolutely settled commerce-clause doctrine. Yet some of the commentary, inside and outside of Congress, treated this choice in a manner that seemed close to charging disingenuousness, putting something of an unmerited cloud around the origin of this profoundly just and in the event most efficacious Public Accommodation Title.

What were the facts and the law? Few things have ever been better proven than that racially discriminative practices very gravely inconvenienced the interstate travel of black people; congressional committee reports established this to the point of absolute demonstration—hardly to the surprise of anybody who knew anything about the subject. You might say, if you landed from Mars and read a dictionary, that "commerce" does not include the movement of human beings, but *Gibbons v. Ogden*,[9] almost a century and a half earlier, had rejected just that argument. Regulations promoting passenger safety and comfort on steamboats had already lived their century. The Interstate Commerce Commission, authorized by Congress under the commerce clause and under that clause alone, had by 1964 been regulating the same subjects, as to railroads, for something like seventy years, and had for a fairly long time been prohibiting on railroads even racial segregation of some sorts, as discriminatory in their effect. One case had actually held that the forcing of black people to move to the back of the bus, when the bus

9. 22 U.S. (9 Wheat) 1 (1824).

passed into a segregating State, imposed an impermissible burden on interstate commerce. The distinction would have had to
be that in these earlier cases the black people were riding on
somebody else's wheels, while in the present case they were
often riding on their own wheels. Can one fault the draftsmen
of the Title for thinking that this was a merely whimsical distinction, obviously trivial in the constitutional context?

As for the jurisdictional base depending on the restaurant's
having received a substantial part of its food from outside the
State, this is an obvious application of the well-established rule
that Congress may prohibit interstate traffic in goods whose
expected use Congress believes to be harmful to the country,
with a slightly different, somewhat closer fitting and more efficient method of enforcement applied to the type of conduct,
interstate shipment plus harmful use, that Congress has dealt
with as a matter of course for a very long time. Not even the
quite untenable and long-abandoned distinction suggested in
Hammer v. Dagenhart,[10] that Congress may act only when the
anticipated harm is in the *receiving* rather than in the *sending*
State, would have faulted this part of the Public Accommodation
Title.

I must add that this commerce clause use has a high esthetic
of its own, worthy, in this context, to compete with the esthetic
of the Fourteenth Amendment. What this Title said was: "The
whole American people have built an integrated nation, whose
parts freely intercommunicate. If you want to make money from
that creation, you may not do so while discriminating, in a materially harmful and morally humiliating manner, against a great
body of citizens within that same American people."

In some of its regions and reaches, the discourse of worry
about the constitutional realities of national power touches
upon one of the many aspects of that rather morose and embit-
tered body of doctrine *manqué* that wears the label "States'

10. 247 U.S. 251 (1918).

rights." It may happen that some factually new federal measure, say, the criminalization of loan-sharking, will be assailed not so much for its being inherently in excess of federal power as for its "invading" concerns "reserved to the several States." The earliest case I know of in which something like this contention was at least implicitly rejected was the 1838 *Coombs* case that I discussed a while ago,[11] the case of the goods stolen off Rockaway Beach; of course the offense, in addition to being a federal offense, was a state crime. The latest case of the same kind that I happen to remember right now is the 1971 *Perez* case,[12] the loan-sharking case just alluded to; New York, again, either did make or might make loan-sharking a crime. This argument always loses, and pretty much always has been a loser, but I think the anomaly commonly found in its invocation is insufficiently attended to. Because, as these two cases, and a near infinitude of others, illustrate, the litigant party interposing a claim of "States' rights" is usually (though there are many exceptions) *not any State*; the records in these cases far more often than not fail to show any *State*'s interest in seeing the Act of Congress fall to the ground. Take *Champion v. Ames*,[13] the 1904 lottery-tickets case. The shipment of lottery tickets was between Texas and California. The defendant's contention was that the regulation of lotteries, and therefore of lottery tickets, was a matter "reserved to the States." Yet the report of the case gives no indication that either Texas or California, as a State, had any objection at all to the national law. Now that is a peculiar position in a lawsuit, no matter how many times we have seen it, no matter how accustomed to it we have grown. I often wonder what the law would have looked like if persons in no way representing any State had not been allowed to plead "States' rights" at all, just as, generally, nobody but me can plead my rights.

11. 37 U.S. (12 Pet.) 72 (1938).
12. Perez v. United States, 402 U.S. 146 (1971).
13. 188 U.S. 321 (1903).

The "States' rights" line of thought hits another snag. The States of the Union are represented, one-by-one and on a basis of equality, in the Senate. Every Act of Congress must have been favored by more of these Senators than disfavored it; often, of course, bills pass by considerably more than a bare majority in the Senate. (And one must allow for the rare case of a tie.) In *Champion v. Ames,* for an example that is also a paradigm, we know that more Senators than not voted for the national law forbidding interstate shipment of lottery tickets. Quite aside from questions of estoppel and waiver, this makes of "States' rights" a two-edged sword, rather sharper on the side that favors the national action than on the negative side. The passage of the Lottery Act showed that the accredited representatives of the States as States favored it; we have no other way of registering, on the national level, the desire and even the constitutional judgment of a State. The States that favored the Lottery Act were claiming the right, as components and constituents of the federal Union, to use their power in the Congress of the Union to keep lottery tickets outside their borders, a thing that, as States, they could not practically do for themselves. The "States' rights" slogan comes into court on both sides of every argument about federal power over persons and events within the States, with at least a slight presumptive weight in favor of the affirmative.

But after and above all, the expansive mode of interpretation of our national constitutional powers is a thing we should be unworried about for intellectual reasons. Our way of interpreting our Constitution, over all the years since 1787, has been the right way. It is the right way because it was what it took to make the Constitution work, and so was guided by the highest canon of constitutional interpretation. It is strikingly shown to be the right way by the intellectual quality of the semi-objections to it that one hears in academic circles. These are now generally marked, I think, by their being merely worried queries, rather than robust and viable alternatives to the road we have gone.

Much of this sort of worrying surrounds the commerce and taxation clauses. There is some talk of "principled" limits to these clauses, but little or no tendering of any actual developed and articulated principles. And it seems not always to be remembered that "principles," to prevail in law, must be not only "principles," but principles actually shown to be *valid,* by preponderance of legal reason. It is against this background that I have chosen to speak of "worrying" about the extent of the national powers, rather than addressing myself to clearly articulated alternatives to the interpretation of those powers that actually marks American constitutional law. I don't seem to find such clearly articulated alternatives. Only worries.

The stress of these worries shows up in many guises. In the *Kahriger*[14] case, for example, wherein the Court sustained a national tax on the occupation of being a professional gambler, Justice Jackson, concurring in the judgment said:

> I concur in the judgment and opinion of the Court, but with such doubt that if the minority agreed upon an opinion which did not impair legitimate using of the taxing power, I probably would join it.[15]

Jackson had an efficaciously and restlessly probing mind. His statement might put a period to worry about the use of general powers, such as those over taxation and commerce, for such ends as to Congress seem good, at least until someone comes along who can do, affirmatively and constructively, what Jackson by implication disclaims power to do.

In the loan-shark case, Justice Stewart took a different and to me far less appealing line. He said:

> In order to sustain this law we would, in my view, have to be able at the least to say that Congress could rationally have concluded that loan sharking is an activity with interstate attributes which distinguish it in some substantial respect from other local

14. United States v. Kahriger, 345 U.S. 22 (1953).
15. *Id.* at 34.

crime. But it is not enough to say that loan sharking is a national problem, for all crime is a national problem. It is not enough to say that some loan sharking has interstate characteristics, for any crime may have an interstate setting. And the circumstance that loan sharking has an adverse impact on interstate business is not a distinguishing attribute, for interstate business suffers from almost all criminal activity, be it shoplifting or violence in the streets.

Because I am unable to discern any rational distinction between loan sharking and other local crime, I cannot escape the conclusion that this statute was beyond the power of Congress to enact.[16]

Now I'm not sure Jusice Stewart was right even in his factual estimate. Testimony before congressional committees seemed to show that some 350 million dollars a year were involved in the loan-sharking business, and that much of this money was serving as working capital for interstate crime. On these facts, I believe I could think of crimes ("flashing," bar-room fisticuffs, incest?) less connected than loan-sharking with national concerns. But my main trouble is with the larger pattern of Stewart's reasoning. He does not say that loan-sharking is unconnected with national concerns. He does not even say that it is not "substantially" connected with national concerns. He seems to be saying that, even if it is so connected, it must be left unregulated because he can't think of anything *less* connected. Would not the indicated conclusion rather be that *all* crime is regulable by the national power? If that were to happen, it would not be because anybody wanted to cheat, or was behaving disingenuously, but because it had turned out that in modern times connections between crime and the national economy and society always exist.

Perhaps the most extreme and stress-induced behavior stimulated by the worry I am thinking about is the tendering of simple imaginary cases about the reach of the powers of the nation. Let one example suffice. Robert Stern asks:

16. 402 U.S. 146, 157–58.

Can Congress forbid the possession or transfer of all pills, or all white pills, because of the difficulty of distinguishing dangerous pills from others and because some might move interstate?[17]

I always refuse my students' requests that I discuss this question, or any others like it, but I always hope they will ask me to do so, because that enables me to get in a valuable point: Such questions are fatally incomplete, Hamlet without the Prince of Denmark, unless we know *why* Congress did what it did; unless we are prepared to perform the task of imagining every state of fact that might underlie and motivate such a legislative measure, then we are talking about nothing. (As to the white pill question, fate has, since its propounding, played quite a trick; after the Tylenol scare, and given the possibility that potassium cyanide may be easier to mix undetected with white materials, and supposing a wide epidemic of such poisonings . . . well, who can say? I'd want to see the Committee reports.)

So if you're among those worried about the expansive mode of interpretation that marks our employment of the national powers, I suggest to you that now, as we prepare for the Constitution's bicentennial, might be a good time to stop worrying. If you're seriously worried, then you're worried about something very serious because, if your worries have any ground, virtually our entire government is suspect of illegitimacy. I think you ought also to consider that the only thing that could have been done about deciding on the legitimacy of our interpretive modes was to submit them to some authority, and that they have been submitted to, and an affirmative answer given by *all* the national authorities we have, *all* the national representatives there are of the conscience and will of the whole American people and of the States one by one. Remember, too, that virtually every interest-group in the country has for a long time insisted on the use of expansively interpreted federal power to serve its

17. *See* Stern, *The Commerce Clause Revisited,* 15 ARIZ. L. REV. 271 (1973).

own ends; your worries have no principled constituency. If your worry takes the "States' rights" form, remember that most cases in which "States' rights" are asserted do not involve any State as a party in interest; that on the whole no bill can get through the Senate without the support of the Senators of more States than oppose it; and that the States who want the federal power to act have their rights too. At least suspend your worry until somebody comes forward with a well-articulated, and above all a well-validated, theory about "principled limits" on, say, the commerce power, something more nutritive and sustaining than the mere wistful yearning for such "principled limits." And whatever you do don't worry over fanciful cases about white pills, or one-eyed donkeys; no instance of the exercise of national power can be evaluated without reference to the shape and size of the national interest actually believed by a *real* Congress to be involved. If you follow the implication of even this last suggestion, I think you'll wait a long time before you worry, because Congress does not, in fact, pass laws that are not substantially related to national interests. Not often enough for you to worry about.

And remember, most indispensably, that worry about the enormous scope and reach of the national powers, the commerce power, the taxing power, the spending power, the admiralty power, and all the rest, most often expresses itself, among thoughtful and disinterested people, as a yearning for "principled limits" on the employment of those powers. But these people seem to have overlooked that there is no lack, but rather an abundance, of such limits, some of them in robust being, some visibly developing, some yet to come into sight. I am referring, of course, to those "limits" that are to be found where limits belong, in the material that Cooley, in the nineteenth century, called "Constitutional Limitations," the material we designate generically as the "Bill of Rights" material, the material that is forming itself, even in our years, into a *system* of human rights capable of much the same creativeness as is exhibited by our system of national empowerments, by broad reading, by analogic reasoning, by reasoning from structure and relationships, by discovery of substantive-law implications in the concept of "citizenship," by the unfolding at last into law of our centrally placed and most ancient commitments, those made in the Declaration of Independence and in the Preamble to the Constitution. If you're worried about the quite real dangers in broad governmental power, I recommend you redirect the energy consumed in worrying about the fact that the United States government has never been and never will be a generally feeble organism, flawed here and there by textual accident, hemmed in by imaginary and quite unvalidated bounds on the exercise of powers stated without bounds. Direct that energy instead toward thought about the limits that exist, by their nature, where limits belong, where they directly and ever more powerfully and creatively can protect the human rights of human beings, as against *all* government power, state and national, and not the interest of an extortionate loan-shark, or a kidnapper, or a polluter of earth, air and water, in being put in jail by one government rather than by another.

Of course there are some people who, in the very teeth of the words of the Ninth Amendment, worry about the legitimacy of the development, under the shield of that Amendment, of a generalized system of human rights. I think there are antidotes to that worry as well. I have just mentioned one very powerful antidote, the perception that there is, to say the least, no reason why our constitutional law of human rights should not grow by the use of interpretive methods as liberalizing and creative as those that have been accepted and employed in our constitutional law of empowerments. There are other antidotes as well. But time does pass, and that will have to be another story.

ON THE FAILURE AND
SUCCESS OF COURTS*

Come with me, in imagination, back to the Seattle of early 1861, just in time for the last news of 1860 to have reached us from the populous East. This news has been long in coming, for the planned Pacific Telegraph will not reach the Coast until later this year.[1] But now we have before us a New York newspaper of December 31, 1860.

What we read opens our minds to grim doubt concerning our own future. The bleak fact is that we are held as the territory of a dissolving nation. What is to happen to us out here? We dimly see many possibilities. Shall we be part of a loose customs-union with some or all of our distant sister states? Will there be a split into two or three confederations—perhaps North and South and West? We have brought here and kept our loyalties to the Union as it was, but may not that Union soon be so changed that incorporation with Canada and the British Empire may after all seem the best step we can plan? None of these possibilities is unrealistic.

So we have to consider—and on long winter evenings we do consider—the condition and history of the United States. Does that Republic seem to be growing toward the kind of na-

*From *The Unfinished Business of the Warren Court,* The Holmes Devise Lectures at the University of Washington Law School, Seattle, in 1970. Originally in the *Washington Law Review,* volume 46, number 3, 1970.
    1. R. THOMPSON, WIRING A CONTINENT 367–68 (1947).

tional character that can reach out to Seattle, nourish and guard Seattle, make Seattle a part of itself?

There are educated people amongst us—a wide reader such as Henry L. Yesler,[2] a man of many lives like David S. Maynard,[3] a doctor who also practices law—people who know a good deal about the political history of the United States, in these days when politics is so eager a preoccupation of all. What has gone wrong (they may ask one another) with the so carefully built and so much praised structure of the Union? Perhaps they may even discuss the part that has been assigned in this structure to the judicial branch. If we get that far, in 1861 Seattle, it may be someone will think of so famous a man as John Marshall. Perhaps one or two people now in Seattle know something of his work. If any of us do, then they can tell the rest of us that the constitutional judgments of Marshall's Court defined, better than any other public utterances have defined, the kind of nation it would take to come and stand strongly on Puget Sound and Elliott Bay, and to make our Seattle wholly a part of itself forever. Seattle needs John Marshall in 1861.

But twenty-five years should suffice for judging the work of a public man, and if we think at all about this man whose judgments could have meant so much to Seattle, we must without reservation pronounce him a failure. Marshall, it can now be seen, followed that *ignis fatuus* most fatally attractive to intellectual man—he sought to create by noble language a structure which reality was all the while rejecting. Seattle must find its future in another kind of structure.

If anyone in our village happens to have had conversation with John Marshall toward the end of the Chief Justice's life— and this is obviously possible, in the case of so accessible a man and so well-traveled a group—and if the Chief Justice was then, as he often was, in a mood for frank talk, then that person may add that Marshall bitterly agreed with this verdict on his work.

2. C. Bagley, Pioneer Seattle and Its Founders 10 (1925).
3. *Id.* at 9 n.2.

He knew that his doctrines had not taken root. Even before he came on the bench, his more famous and powerful fellow-Virginians, Jefferson and Madison, had espoused notions of "interposition" quite irreconcilable with nationhood. In the late 'twenties and early 'thirties, "nullification" had taken off the "interposition" mask, and had found its greatest but by no means lonely theorist in Calhoun. When Marshall showed signs of acting against genocide in Georgia, against the planned smashing to bits of a civilized Indian tribe, his interventions were rejected as impudent and were successfully defied, with the acquiescence of the President.[4] It is true that Jackson, in the nearly contemporary nullification controversy involving South Carolina and the tariff, spoke the language of national supremacy, but what value was there in a sporadic enforcement of national law, according to Presidential preference?[5] In any case, as Beveridge is later to say, "The net result was that nullification triumphed,"[6] for the tariff act was drastically modified in 1833, as a direct result of South Carolina's threat of disobedience. John Marshall died a crushed man.

Now, in Seattle village of 1861, twenty-five years later, it is very plain that Marshall did right to despair. He built on the concept of one people. The people of the Union are two peoples, with a third voiceless people in slavery. Nobody cares about national supremacy, or broadly defined national power, as things in themselves; people care about less abstract issues, and use these two ideas when they help, flouting them when they hinder.[7] Now the threatened news has come. South Carolina has left the Union, and other States are sure to follow.

Through these same twenty-five years, the Supreme Court has built little on Marshall's foundations. Here in Seattle, in

4. *See* Worcester v. Georgia, 31 U.S. (6 Pet.) 515 (1832); *see generally* 4 A. BEVERIDGE, THE LIFE OF JOHN MARSHALL 539–52 (1919).
5. *See* E. PESSEN, JACKSONIAN AMERICA 198 (1969).
6. 4 A. BEVERIDGE, *supra* note 4, at 574.
7. *See, e.g.,* 2 C. WARREN, THE SUPREME COURT IN UNITED STATES HISTORY 290 (Rev. ed. 1926).

1861, we will probably be as unsuccessful as later generations are to be in arriving at a satisfactory evaluation of the Taney Court. But we do know one thing, and in that one thing all else is merged. In the *Dred Scott*[8] case, the Court has said that the national government flatly lacks constitutional power to deal with the chief national question—the question of slavery in the territories. That is what has happened, on the Court, to *Gibbons v. Ogden*[9] and *McCulloch v. Maryland*.[10] Those cases projected national power adequate and apt to national need. *Dred Scott,* applying the narrowing-interpretation techniques which were anathema to Marshall's mind and death to his vision, says the nation has not even the power to save itself *in extremis.*

Maybe I have overdrawn on the political knowledge of the settlers of Seattle in 1861. What reading I have been able to do on the backgrounds of some of them leads me to doubt this. But if they knew even a little about John Marshall's constitutional work, they knew that that work had utterly failed. The system he had built in his mind was just right for Seattle. But Seattle, as of 1861, is going to have to content itself with something more tuned to the ethos of the Union's people, something less perfect but more feasible, something—if I may lapse anachronistically into the cant of our own '60's—more "relevant."

In late 1861, the Pacific Telegraph reaches San Francisco,[11] and news comes to us a little faster. And what surprising news, as the next years go on! No one, I think, knows why the North decided to fight, and fought on in the face of defeat, and gave 675,000 lives; the secret is dispersed with the ashes of bonfires on village greens, with the echoes of sober conversations among families and friends. There must have been something in unconsciousness, waiting for the sound of a trumpet. However it happened, the news of Appomattox at last reached Seattle.

8. Dred Scott v. Sandford, 60 U.S. (19 How.) 393 (1857).
9. 22 U.S. (9 Wheat.) 1 (1824).
10. 17 U.S. (4 Wheat.) 316 (1819).
11. R. THOMPSON, *supra* note 1, at 367–68.

Washington Territory was not lacking in lawyers.[12] Some of them must have been reminded of John Marshall's splendid nationalist judgments. In your beautiful Seattle phrase, perhaps in use even in those days, the mountain was out.

Now the Marshall Court, as all know, is the paradigm of judicial success. I have tried to show what an abysmal and final failure it must have seemed in 1861, here in an outpost to which its success was supremely important. The failure occurred because, in 1861, it was plain that John Marshall had misread the national character. The paradigmatic success that finally emerged came because what was plain in 1861 was altogether untrue and had been untrue from the beginning. Lincoln and Antietam did not happen after 1861. They were there already. John Marshall became the archetype of success because all along, against all seeming, in spite even of his own despair, he had correctly read the deepest impulses of the nation, and the destiny toward which those impulses were to lead it.

The Warren Court is now just dissolved, and the urge to evaluate its place in history is nearly irresistible. What question can we meaningfully ask, now?

The first thing is to arrive at some overall strategic approximation to a statement of what the Warren Court has been about. Here there is considerable though not insuperable difficulty.

The difficulties arise in part from the fact that—unlike the Marshall Court—the Warren Court has not spoken with a single voice. The habits of dissent and of separate concurrence have grown since Marshall's time. A second difficulty, connected with the first, is that the Warren Court has contained many strong figures, not by any means all like-minded. Then, thirdly, changes in personnel have resulted in changes in direction, in the taking of new tacks, and even in some retreats.

---

12. *See* A. Beardsley, Controversies Over Location of the Seat of Government in Washington 284 (1941), *reprinted from* 32 Pacific Northwest Quarterly 239, 401 (1941).

I wish I had the training to study to some effect the fascinating problem in decisional dynamics presented by this Court's history. The process by which it has brought the law so far will never yield its secret to counting, in simplistic categories such as "liberal" and "conservative." There has been at work, instead, a most complicated set of interactions. Mr. Justice Clark, sometimes spoken of as though he were consistently conservative, wrote for the Court in a number of chain-breaking decisions— *Mapp v. Ohio*,[13] *Hamm v. Rock Hill*,[14] and *Burton v. Wilmington Parking Authority*;[15] characterized in the New York Times story on his retirement as conservative on civil rights,[16] he was in fact reliably anti-racist. Mr. Justice Stewart, whom many think of as relatively traditionalist, wrote the opinion that emancipated the thirteenth amendment and gave it room to grow into a general law on all the incidents and badges and consequences of slavery.[17] Mr. Justice White wrote for the Court the most advanced of its "state action" opinions—*Reitman v. Mulkey*[18]—and contributed from the lawyer-like quality of his mind to legitimation of the result in *Evans v. Newton*.[19] Mr. Justice Harlan gave the support of his careful general conservatism to the result in what is probably the most advanced of the Court's doctrinal motions—the judgment in *Griswold v. Connecticut*.[20] On the other hand, no Justice has been found always on the side which the public would classify as "liberal." The Warren Court was a body

13. 367 U.S. 643 (1961).
14. 379 U.S. 306 (1964).
15. 365 U.S. 715 (1961).
16. N.Y. Times, March 1, 1967, at 1, col. 6.
17. Jones v. Alfred H. Mayer Co., 392 U.S. 409 (1968). I ought in candor to say that I cannot agree with the Court's interpretation of the 1866 statute in this case, though for other reasons not now requiring rehearsal I think the case rightly decided. The important thing about *Jones* is its recognition of Section 2 of the thirteenth amendment as a source of wide Congressional power—and its clear implication that the Amendment of its own force does more than merely abolish chattel slavery.
18. 387 U.S. 369 (1967).
19. 382 U.S. 296 (1966).
20. 381 U.S. 479 (1965).

of strong-minded independent men, each sensitively conscious of his individual responsibility, but whose dynamic interaction somehow added up to a strong thrust in an at least vaguely identifiable direction. When time has unlocked the documents, students of the decisional process will have here a uniquely interesting course of events to study.

For all this complexity, we would be wrong not to see in the work of the Warren Court, as a matter of net thrust, an affirmation—the strongest, by a very long interval, in our whole history—of the positive content and worth of American citizenship. Without making this lecture a catalogue of cases, I will invite your own reflection on what I would take to be the structure of American citizenship as the Warren Court has projected it and filled it in—sometimes with a feeling of obviousness in the product, and sometimes with that "sublime audacity"[21] which has been praised in John Marshall, and which often goes into the making of good law.

First, citizenship is the right to be heard and counted on public affairs, the right to vote on equal terms,[22] to speak,[23] and to hold office when legitimately chosen.[24] Concomitant to and enveloping these rights is the right to associate for political purposes.[25] Alexander Meiklejohn long ago taught us that the citizen is as much a part of government, as definitely an empow-

21. 4 A. BEVERIDGE, *supra* note 4, at 302.
22. Baker v. Carr, 369 U.S. 186 (1962), and its sequel cases. I have to say that I cannot go all the way with the Court in its imposition of mathematically precise equality across the board. *See* Black, *Representation in Law and Equity,* IN REPRESENTATION 131 (Pennock & Chapman eds. 1968). But the excesses, if they are that, are minor and correctable, while the pre-*Baker* position was intolerable.
23. New York Times Co. v. Sullivan, 376 U.S. 254 (1964) is perhaps the greatest landmark. It is worth noting, however, that in United States v. Robel, 389 U.S. 258 (1967), the Court finally threw the last shovelful of earth on the theory that the first amendment is not "law" by squarely holding unconstitutional an Act of Congress under that amendment.
24. Powell v. McCormack, 395 U.S. 486 (1969); Bond v. Floyd, 385 U.S. 116 (1966).
25. Shelton v. Tucker, 364 U.S. 479 (1960).

ered component in government, as is any official;[26] in a recent book of my own, I have argued that from this mere status much of what we derive from the first amendment could have been derived even if there had been no first amendment.[27] This public aspect of citizenship has been strongly firmed into law by the Warren Court.

Secondly, citizenship means the right to be treated fairly when one is the object of action by that government of which one is also a part. Continual expansion is of the essence here, for no procedure is ever fair enough. The Warren Court has effected great expansion,[28] and, even more important, has put in our hands the conceptual means for further growth. The change effected is one of kind rather than of degree, for the Warren Court has finally cast aside the methodological canons that would bound this part of citizenship by narrow historical considerations, and has given our legal culture a new freedom to search out and destroy the blight of rightlessness, wherever it may spread.

Thirdly, citizenship is the broad right to lead a *private* life— for without this all dignity and happiness are impossible, and public rights mere futilities. The Warren Court has powerfully affirmed this aspect of citizenship—as to marriage,[29] as to religion,[30] as to travel[31]—and has given us methodologic tools for extending it wherever it should be extended.

This citizenship of three interconnected aspects should be enough. But to this triad, defining as it does the good political life, the Warren Court has added one more thing—a thing our

26. A. Meiklejohn, Free Speech and Its Relation to Self-Government (1948).

27. C. Black, Structure and Relationship in Constitutional Law 35–51 (1969).

28. Citation seems idle; the names of the cases are a proud legion.

29. Loving v. Virginia, 388 U.S. 1 (1967); Griswold v. Connecticut, 381 U.S. 479 (1965).

30. Abington School Dist. v. Schempp, 374 U.S. 203 (1963); Engel v. Vitale, 370 U.S. 421 (1962).

31. Aptheker v. Secretary of State, 378 U.S. 500 (1964).

history made it sadly necessary to add. It has affirmed, as no Court before it ever did, that this three-fold citizenship is to be enjoyed in all its parts without respect to race, "as far as constitutional law can accomplish it"—the long-unhonored promise of the *Slaughter-House Cases*.[32]

I would expand here a little, though not to full extension, my belief, elsewhere expressed,[33] that filling with content the concept of citizenship need not result in neglect of the rights of aliens among us. I think just the opposite to be true—that the rights of the lawfully resident alien ought to be measured by the rights of the citizen, with only such exceptions as definite history or *nationally* determined necessity may dictate, in strict subjection to the Bill of Rights. I should think that it may one day be squarely held, as it has already been suggested, that the whole subject of alienage is constitutionally preempted to the nation,[34] and that no state may take any action adverse to aliens as such, save for the historically and textually validated exceptions of voting and office-holding. I should think that once the nation has decided that a man may live here, that decision implies by plain necessity a decision that he may live in some state, and that a state's putting him (except with respect to these political rights) on a different footing from its other residents amounts to diminution by a state of that which the nation, for its own purposes, has given—an action no more to be countenanced than would the discriminatory taxation by a state of foreign imports as such.[35] As to national action respecting aliens, the relevant parts of the Bill of Rights, and inferentially all the radiations and penumbrae of the Bill of Rights, protect all "persons." But this is an excursus, and I shall leave it at that, except to say that it is a part of the unfinished business of the Warren Court.

32. 83 U.S. (16 Wall.) 36 (1873).
33. C. BLACK, *supra* note 27, at 64.
34. *See* Hines v. Davidowitz, 312 U.S. 52 (1941).
35. *See* Brown v. Maryland, 25 U.S. (12 Wheat.) 419 (1827).

Now if I am right in this overall characterization of the triadic citizenship the Warren Court has worked to establish, what question should we be asking about that Court?

If the Marshall Court is the paradigm of success, then perhaps the mode through which it became that may be the paradigm of evaluation. I took a look the other day at the well-written article on Marshall in a volume of the ENCYCLOPEDIA AMERICANA published in 1854.[36] His early career is sketched in detail. His service as Chief Justice is lauded in general terms. But there is not a word about any of his constitutional judgments, or even (except for one quite vague hint) about his place as a constitutional judge. How did this article get revised?

It took a lot of time. Constitutional doctrine succeeds if it expresses what turn out to be at last the authentic impulses of the nation. If I have rightly, though vaguely, caught the true characterization of the Warren Court, then we shall have to wait and see—and we should be extremely wary of accepting the fashions and feelings of one day, or of one or ten or twenty years, for that which may at length assert itself.

Closely connected is another point. Even within the political structure narrowly considered, no Court succeeds alone. *McCulloch v. Maryland*[37] and *Gibbons v. Ogden*[38] constructed a frame ample to any national need. But those cases would be dead today—mere antiquarian curiosities—if Congress and the President and the people had not taken the leads they gave, used the powers they validated, and accepted that use as legitimate. Declared constitutional rights will not be enjoyed unless people will litigate on them to judgment, and unless the judgments are supported by the other branches of government. They will not be enjoyed—and here I speak to the immediate and longer future—if lawyers will not show a *constans et perpetua voluntas* to

36. ENCYCLOPEDIA AMERICANA, MARSHALL (Vethake ed., Supp. Vol. 1854).
37. 17 U.S. (4 Wheat.) 316 (1819).
38. 22 U.S. (9 Wheat.) 1 (1824).

guard them against practical as well as conceptual circumvention.

There is another thing to be learned from the failure of the Marshall Court, and the events that followed it. In virtually contemporary sizing-up of the success of any Court, it is a delicate task indeed—I am inclined to think an impossible one, in its effect if not in its intent—to distinguish between evaluation and desire. The wrongness, inadaptability, failure of a Court's work are questions rather than observations, and they are questions about the future, and so they easily become questions about one's own hopes rather than questions about what one is evaluating. If one were talking about the Marshall Court in, say, 1858, such phrases as "proved unworkable" or "merely visionary" would seem inevitably to contain implications as to one's own position in a battle still being fought.

There is therefore only one thing I would say confidently, now, about the Warren Court. It is the only Court so far in American history which has so much as a chance of being one day thought as great as the Marshall Court, for it is the only Court that has made an assertion as large as the Marshall Court made. Marshall took a set of disconnected texts and read them together in the light of an overall vision of nationhood. The Warren Court—and this is its distinctive achievement in method—decisively and one may hope finally has rejected that mode of reading our constitutional guarantees, both substantive and procedural, as though each were a narrow thing-in-itself, to be grudgingly construed, and has insisted that these guarantees, readable in themselves, in their radiations, and in their interstices, are to be looked on as forming a total scheme of citizenship. The Warren Court (not, to be sure without honored antecedents, as Marshall's work was not without antecedents) perceived in these guarantees a pervading systemic equity, an equity of respect for the citizen, and thus set in full motion a way of looking at them which can make of their totality a plan adequate, in shape and size, to confront Marshall's plan of nationhood.

Marshall wove his firm-textured dream of *one* people. In his day, state particularism was the unresting threat to that dream. But was it merely an accident that state particularism, where at its most virulent, where it strained and then broke the Union, was built around the most drastic possible denial of equality and freedom? Could, or *can,* a *nation* endure half slave and half free?

I think it plain that we will not be or remain a nation worth calling a nation unless we plant ourselves on the moral ground to which the Warren Court has given its outlines—not in all the details of all the decisions of that Court, but following the broad lines the Warren Court has laid out. We need this moral basis of citizenship—common, growing citizenship—as we need cleaner water and air. It is conceivable that there may exist some-time, somewhere, a national state with no other vocation than the modest one of preserving itself. But we have a different birth from that; we live congenitally under a different and inescapable commandment; we have stood together at the foot of the moun-tain. If a sense of rightness and mission is a thing we need so as to be able to face the future, and if extension to all of that three-part citizenship which I have outlined is the only mission to which we can worthily give ourselves, then the Warren Court, like the Marshall Court, has been trying to make us a nation.

I have made a large claim for the Warren Court—the largest possible against the background of our history. I have asserted that there was set to us, in our beginning, a task that is not two but one—the task of making a nation, based on the consent and will of one people, wherein full citizenship should prevail for all. If this is right, then in the joint company of John Marshall and Earl Warren we are questing after a nationhood with moral meaning and purpose, after a political society as good as politics can make it. For that society, even for the earnest attempt to build it, we can give E. M. Forster's "Two Cheers,"[39] reserving three cheers, as he did, for the society which politics alone can

39. E. FORSTER, TWO CHEERS FOR DEMOCRACY 70 (1951).

never create. All here will die before we know how it comes out. Indeed, such things never finally come out. For us, as for all people, the search is the Grail.

I asked a little while ago what might be the right question to put to ourselves about the Warren Court, as it steps back into the shadows of time. The question with meaning, the realistic question, the answerable question, is not whether the Warren Court succeeded. It is not even whether, in the Seattle of 1993, where, if I am spared and blessed, I shall bring grandchildren to ride that quaint old Monorail, it will be thought to have succeeded; sometimes even tentative success takes longer than that, as the posthumous history of the Marshall Court shows. The answerable question, the question that hard realism asks, is whether we want to make it succeed.

It has been said that the South surrendered at Appomattox to John Marshall.[40] Then it is not too much to say that in one generation, willingly and unwillingly, for the most part unknowingly, 675,000 people died to make reality of the rhetoric of *Cohens v. Virginia*.[41] If in the coming generation 675,000 people were to dedicate themselves, willingly and knowingly, to making the Warren Court succeed—particularly if a few thousand were to be young lawyers of skill and dedication—then I tremblingly predict that in Seattle in this law school in 1993, twenty-five years after Earl Warren's stepping down, people will be saying that the Warren Court, for all their difference in style and decisional dynamics, was comparable in greatness to the Marshall Court.

40. JOHN MARSHALL: LIFE, CHARACTER AND JUDICIAL SERVICES xiii (J. Dillon ed. 1903).
41. 19 U.S. (6 Wheat.) 264 (1821). Rereading that opinion, and having recently had occasion (see note 39, *supra*) to go over the main events in Marshall's life, I cannot keep myself from recording my lively distaste (I had almost chosen a stronger word) for what has become a thing of frequent occurrence—the patronizing and light ridiculing of the work and style of such a man, by persons who are so many untravellable leagues from having dared as much and done as much as he, and could not write in a style as good for their century as his was for his, if they had labored at it from childhood all through every day and prayed for it every night.

I have spoken of young laywers because what will be required of us, above all, is *advocacy*. It has often been pointed out
that skilled and tireless advocacy, returning again and again to
insist on the rightness of its cause, can make new law. What we
need now to understand, and to act upon, is the associated truth
that advocacy can also guard and sustain law. It can even bring
it about that retreat, where retreat is compelled, not become
rout, and that there be left behind, for the uses of a better day,
indestructible monuments like the great dissents of Brandeis.
The law of the Warren Court is on the whole a law of political
health and wisdom, worth the most earnest sustaining advocacy,
and sustainable if that advocacy is forthcoming. The management of this legacy, the prevention of its dissipation, so eagerly
anticipated by so many, will be the new challenge to creative
advocacy in our next years.

Good law continually refines its reasons, and it will be a
vital component in the sustaining advocacy of these coming
years to refine continually the reason behind the constitutional
law the Warren Court has formed. This will be the answer—the
only possible answer and the sufficient answer—to the recurrent
charge of want of "principle" in the Warren Court decisions.
That charge has been multifarious. In part, it is no more than
a call for something unattainable in any working law at any
time—total logical consistency not only of enunciated rules but
of rules thought likely to be enunciated with respect to imagined
future cases. In this aspect, the call for "principle" is but old
mechanical jurisprudence writ large, or small, and it is sufficient
to say that one hundred years of jurisprudential rejections of
this mode of thought only put in bold relief the tragedy of its
being wheeled up again to cast a shadow on results of the most
evident justice. Much of this critique ignores the fact, plain as
a pikestaff, that any viable legal system has different methods
and styles, as well as different rules, for different problem-areas.
We do not even treat real property and personal property just
alike; we treat marital rights and riparian rights very differently

indeed. On the other hand, some of the worst mistakes in any legal system come from insufficient inconsistency; in our own case, one sore instance, productive of injustice and suffering, is our treating a housewife as though she were a banker, for the purpose of defining the consequences of her making a promissory note. On analysis, too, the question of "principle" often turns out to be merely an ordinary lawyers' question about the sufficiency of a distinction. Religious differences, race differences, age differences, political differences, and sex differences are not the same, either with respect to the facts or with respect to the relevant constitutional texts, and there is no across-the-board a priori reason why they should be treated as though they were the same. The intellectual soundness of a constitutional system may quite as likely be shown in its differentiating one kind of discrimination from another—or in its devising evidentiary or remedial rules which are applicable to one but not to the other—as by its lumping them together. If the life of the law has been experience, then experience teaches that tolerable solutions to the problems of law are rarely attainable by the utterance and Procrustean application of huge generalizations. Tolerable solutions, morever, are not attainable, never have been attainable, and never will be attainable if justice must wait until answers are given to every question intellectual curiosity can suggest as to the reaches and connections of every rule.

I make bold to quote, moreover, from Plucknett, on an important phase in the development of English law: "[T]hose sweeping and violent social revolutions which occurred in Switzerland and France were avoided in English history through the slow adaptation of the law to new social conditions, no doubt assisted by the lack of a precise definition of property, while the willingness to tolerate for a time a few anomalies helped to accomplish by peaceful means the great task of transforming the ancient serfdom into a class of free workers."[42] A legal system

42. T. PLUCKNETT, A CONCISE HISTORY OF THE COMMON LAW 34 (5th ed. 1956).

in process of change will not move at a uniform rate, nor find *instanter* its new reason to the last decimal place. Those who insist it must are insisting on paralysis.

At the same time, reason is an essential component in the art of law—reason supporting justice, reason subtly and flexibly adapting itself to the gross and fine-grained differences in life. In the end, it is quite true that the work of the Warren Court will endure only if our own later work can support it with that kind of reason, the only kind good law ever has or needs. This process of continual reworking and search will surely result in some changes in rule and in outcome—in some contractions and in some expansions. But if the great changes effected by the Court are in the direction of a justice consonant with our national ethos—and I believe they are—then the reasoned system will be constructed and refined that can contain them.

CONSTITUTIONAL PROBLEMS IN
COMPULSORY "NATIONAL SERVICE"*

I have been asked to talk about the constitutionality of compulsory national service, discussed but not recommended in the report of the Commission on Selective Service. Proposals for compulsory non-military service by young people show a considerable variety among themselves, and this variety gives to any constitutional discussion a tentative and very general character. But those proposals which I have seen would in some way require that those young men, or perhaps even those young people, who are not selected for military service, enter, for a period of two or three years, some other kind of national, state or community training or service.

It may be needless to say that only the *compulsory* feature of these proposals raises serious constitutional issues. I cannot think that our Constitution inhibits us from tendering opportunities to our young people; the constitutional problems—and the very serious problems of policy—arise when we consider saying to these young people that they must accept one of the tendered opportunities or go to jail.

There is the Thirteenth Amendment. It seems, at first reading, that a distinction between "involuntary service," which is certainly the thing proposed, and "involuntary servitude," which the Thirteenth Amendment forbids, is too delicate to live in a constitutional atmosphere. In the Fourth Article of the

*Yale Law Report, volume 13, number 3, 1967. Copyright Yale University 1967.

Constitution, the word "service" is used to refer to the very thing principally referred to in the Amendment. Of course, a national service system is not the thing centrally intended, as a matter of history. It was Negro slavery that held the center of the stage. But constitutional phrases of this sort are almost never held to the narrow scope of the central emphasis in the minds of those who first uttered them. And the Supreme Court has held the Amendment to cover other forms of involuntary servitude. For example, in *Pollock v. Williams*, a 1944 decision, the Court strongly reiterated its prior holdings that the Amendment forbade even an indirect attempt to punish the non-performance of a labor contract. A good many state courts have refused equitable enforcement of contracts for personal services, either by applying the Amendment itself or by stating a public policy worded in identical or indistinguishable language. The Pollock Court said that the aim of the Amendment was "not merely to end slavery but to maintain a system of completely free and voluntary labor throughout the United States."

To this principle there have been admitted, necessarily, exceptions based on history. The clearest and most important of these is the military draft. At this point I would suggest to you that the root-idea to which we ought to recur, in dealing with any suggested analogy from the draft, is that, in our public policy and in our constitutionalism, military service is and ought to be a striking, even a startling, exception, and not a thing which can readily be used for founding arguments by analogy. If one uses the military draft as an analogical basis for other invasions of personal freedom, then it seems evident that almost anything can be justified. Time forces me to make this point assertively, without briefing it, but I nevertheless emphasize it and commend it to your consideration. Either military service is an exception, a clearly delimited exception, from which analogical and *a fortiori* arguments may not be made, or there are few if any practical constitutional restraints in the government's dealing with our persons, whether we are 18, 8 or 80.

Beyond the military service, there are many other historical exceptions of a quite different order of magnitude—jury service and the like. The most interesting case here is *Butler v. Perry,* a 1915 decision. The Court held, on historical grounds, that the Thirteenth Amendment did not prevent a state's requiring a few days work on the roads, each year, from its able-bodied citizens. This case—and I think the same may be said of the other exceptions that have been allowed—is clearly and broadly distinguishable from the prepared National Service plan.

First, the exception is historically warranted, whereas National Service would be a bold innovation. Secondly, what was exacted was a small amount of personal service in the course of a normally free life, while National Service would uproot young people and force them into a total pattern of life and labor, for a term of years.

On the whole, with that tentativeness which ought to qualify a just-begun constitutional discussion, I would think the principle of the Thirteenth Amendment ought to be held to rule out compulsory National Service.

At this point I think I must read from the discussion of Secretary Wirtz, who has appeared as an advocate of National Service, for his ideas on coercion introduce another constitutional problem. The Secretary, in a talk that has been widely reproduced, first sketched the opportunities for training and service which might be made available to young people. Then he turns to the less pleasant subject of coercion. He first says that he would be content to try a voluntary plan. But he goes on, and I am quoting selectively from a short passage, but I hope without distortion or omission of any significant qualifying idea:

> There are strong reasons at the same time, for beginning to think through the possibilities of a firmer, tougher course.
>
> It would be precisely those who present the most serious problems, both for themselves and for the community, who would fail

to take advantage of any or all of the options which were offered them; and their continuing derelictions and misdemeanors would make a new system seem not to be working even if it were in fact improving the general situation materially.

There is a point at which the community's good sense has to be asserted—as it is now in the case of education up to age sixteen—with respect to someone who has clearly established his lack of any sense, or any sense of responsibility, at all. And that point is not necessarily, or even wisely, after he has committed a serious offense. The compulsory education concept could very sensibly be extended to cover types of training and discipline better suited to the "hard cases"—not as part of the penal system but as part of the educational system, and yet operated on the community's terms, not the boy's. . . .

The figures showing over 50% of all military draftees being rejected for military service because of their physical or mental condition are not going to be accepted, furthermore, as reflecting a condition which enough of those boys can be expected to straighten out in their own way—even if help is extended to them. We know now from disillusioning experience how few of them will voluntarily accept such help.

There is a cancer here, and the country is ready for surgery.

If it is ready, too, to offer full opportunity, its insistence on commensurate responsibility is not unreasonable.

It is possible today, for the first time in American history, to give every new member of it the opportunity to prepare himself, or herself, for useful lifetime membership. It becomes then a fair bargain that the affording of this opportunity warrants insistence on the obligation to use it.

I would like to be able not to find in these passages two disturbing ideas. The first is that a boy who does not want to go into some form of communally or nationally organized service is presumptively delinquent. "Disturbing" is too weak a word for the idea that in America we no longer have any room for the loner, the maverick, for the boy who feels distaste for authoritative organization of his work and life. Such a boy is not only a delinquent but so thorough an ingrate that we are justified in insisting that he accept willy-nilly the opportunity we tender.

The second idea raises problems more evidently of a constitutional kind, for it is that, having so identified this delinquent, we are to impose a corrective regime on him without waiting for him to do anything wrong. I say this raises constitutional problems, in the plural, and I rejoice that I am addressing men and women of law, because I cannot explore them, but must simply ask you to let the concept of due process play on such a picture.

These things, I sorrowfully must conclude, are what the Secretary has said. I hope—and in some sort believe—that they are not what he means. But I can certainly say that a program whose coercion was rested on such a theory would have to deal, and I hope unsuccessfully, with very serious constitutional problems quite aside from the Thirteenth Amendment.

I want to turn now from the constitutional objections which might be made to such a plan as a whole, to the constitutional difficulties which would arise in its administration.

"Coercion" is a hard word, meaning hard things. To coerce participation in National Service, we would have to tender the alternative of jail. But that would be only the beginning of difficulty. For what is proposed must involve the formation of a huge corps of teen-agers, living in groups, in many cases at least away from their homes, a life which some of them did not choose, and which many of them are likely to find irksome as time passes. In such a situation, offenses must needs come, and I should think in some volume. The military establishment has the system of courts-martial. But how could we justify, constitutionally, the extension of this system to civilian workers or trainees? If a soldier is absent without leave, he is court-martialed. If a National Service worker were similarly absent, it would seem that any serious penalty must be inflicted only after trial by jury, with all the safeguards available in every civilian case, including trained legal counsel at every stage. Could a work program for teen-agers be run this way? And, of course, I am only hinting at the manifold constitutional difficulties.

Now, I think, sooner or later, somebody is going to suggest that there is still a way. In some manner or another, the military draft itself might be used to coerce, indirectly but effectively, participation in the National Service program. You can imagine the different ways in which this might be done—by holding up the military draft as a threatened alternate to entry, by drafting all who ceased to cooperate after they had entered, and so on. It might even be suggested, though I hope it will not be, that Congress could provide for a universal draft, and then in effect parole those not needed in or really eligible for military service into civilian work groups.

Even this might not work. If the subterfuge were palpable enough (and anything so large-scale would be hard to conceal) the courts might not swallow it. But it is true that the Supreme Court ought to and traditionally does defer to Congress on the nature and size of the military establishment, and some use of the military draft to coerce non-military service might be devised, so sophisticated as to force the Court to go along with it.

I suggest to you that such a development would be most unfortunate. The use of mere fictions for supporting a course of action which very probably would violate the Thirteenth Amendment is a thing which it seems we ought to reject simply on hearing the issue stated. Or, at another and more realistic level, if it can reasonably be thought that this "National Service," standing in the open, would violate the Thirteenth Amendment, then the least Congress ought to do is to put it in the open, without protecting fictions, so that the processes of law may determine on the merits, unembarrassed by presumptions suitable only to real military determinations, whether the claim of unconstitutionality has substance.

I will close by restating only one idea that, in my mind, summarizes the whole case, whether of constitutionalism or of policy. Large-scale coercion of labor is foreign to our traditions and to our Constitution. To this generalization, iron necessity has forced us to admit one massive exception—military draft. It is absolutely essential, whether to sound policy or to constitutionalism of the spirit as well as of the letter, that we insulate this exception as an exception, and resist every temptation to use it, by analogy or by way of indirect coercion, as a basis for overthrowing the fundamental policy itself.

THE FAITHLESS ELECTOR:
A CONTRACTS PROBLEM*

Availing myself of the marvelous freedom of this format, I am going to put an idea down here, as briefly as possible. I do not know whether this idea has been expressed by anyone else before. If it has, it cannot hurt for it to get another exposure; if it has not, it certainly should be put forward well before 1980.

Our electoral college system for electing the President sometimes generates the problem of the "faithless elector"—the elector who runs as a member of a slate pledged to vote for a particular candidate, but who casts his vote for somebody else.

I happened to be around Congress and in the galleries when this question came up in January, 1969.[1] One Dr. Bailey, an elector in North Carolina, was pledged to Richard Nixon but voted for George Wallace. The Congress faithfully followed the stage directions in 3 U.S.C. §§15–17.[2] When North Carolina was reached, and the problem of Dr. Bailey was raised, the Houses dissolved their joint session and each met separately (without any further time for research or preparation) for the

---

*Originally published in the *Louisiana Law Review,* volume 38, 1977. Copyright Louisiana State University 1977.
1. *See* 115 CONG. REC. 145–72, 197–246 (1969).
2. 3 U.S.C. §§ 15–17 (1970). These sections provide for a joint session of the Senate and House of Representatives to count electoral votes. If at least one Senator *and* one Representative should object to a particular elector's vote, each house shall meet separately to rule on the objection; unless *both* houses vote to reject the contested vote, it is counted as cast.

two hours, and not a minute more, mandated by section 17,[3] with each member limited to a single five minutes' speech. After this deliberation, if so hectically hurried a "debate" can be called that, each House voted to receive Dr. Bailey's vote as cast, and to count it for Wallace. Reconvening together, they acted accordingly.

This amount of consideration, for a great constitutional question whose solution might determine the identity of the President, could not be thought to rise to the level of frivolity— except for the fact that in the given case Nixon won no matter how you counted Bailey's vote. (My friend, Congressman Bob Eckhardt, said the most sensible thing said on this occasion— in effect that the job of Congress was not to adjudicate issues of no present pragmatic relevance, but to decide who had been elected President, and that Congress should simply have left the "faithless elector" question where it was and declared Nixon to be elected no matter how Bailey's vote was counted.[4])

I decline to believe that such perfunctory consideration of a question, the answer to which made no difference at the time, could determine for all time the right answer to that question when its answer *does* make all the difference, as sometime it easily may. So I have kept thinking, off and on, about the matter.

It struck me the other day—and this is the whole of my idea for this piece—that the problem of the "faithless elector" is a problem, primarily, not of constitutional law but of contract law.

The law of contract is after all the law we customarily think of when we consider what to do about broken promises. If there are firm evidentiary grounds for holding that an elector has made an express or implied-in-fact promise to vote for X (and if there are not the problem cannot arise), and if voters have voted for him in reliance on that promise, then it seems to me that a contract, with valuable and lawful consideration, has been made between him and them, the tenor of which is that he will

3. *Id.* § 17.
4. 115 CONG. REC. 164 (1969).

perform a single, simple act, of a unique value not commensurable with money. This contract falls within familiar categories: It is (as my description of it makes clear) a classic case for the equitable remedy of specific performance; how could the "remedy at law" (money damages) be "adequate"? It is, quite clearly, a third-party beneficiary contract, with the candidate in the role of beneficiary, and modern contracts law generally acknowledges the right of such a beneficiary.

The only substantive question remaining is whether such a contract is "against public policy," and hence void. At this point, of course, we reach a facet of confrontation between contracts law and constitutional law. But how transformed is the constitutional question! The question is not now whether article II of the Constitution,[5] in and of itself, compels the elector to keep his promise, or frees him to break it. The question is rather (and in stating it fairly I think I virtually answer it) whether a promise of a sort *not forbidden* by article II, and regularly made and kept by electors in every article II election for the last century and a half at least, is "against public policy," so as to be unenforceable, notwithstanding its meeting all technical re-

5. U.S. CONST. art. II § 1 provides, in pertinent part:
    Each State shall appoint, in such Manner as the Legislature thereof may direct, a Number of Electors, equal to the whole Number of Senators and Representatives to which the State may be entitled in the Congress. . . .
    The Electors shall meet in their respective States, and vote by Ballot for two Persons, of whom one at least shall not be an Inhabitant of the same State with themselves. And they shall make a List of all the Persons voted for, and of the Number of Votes for each; which List they shall sign and certify, and transmit sealed to the Seat of the Government of the United States, directed to the President of the Senate. The President of the Senate shall, in the Presence of the Senate and the House of Representatives, open all the Certificates, and the Votes shall then be counted. . . .
    The Congress may determine the Time of chusing the Electors, and the Day on which they shall give their Votes; which Day shall be the same throughout the United States.
The twelfth amendment, adopted in 1804 to modify article II insofar as the election of the Vice President was concerned, left the above provisions intact.

166 THE FAITHLESS ELECTOR

quirements of contract law. I do think that question pretty well answers itself; certainly I can think of no better way to argue it than merely to state it.

There remain questions of procedure for enforcement of this contract. I would hope that it will not be thought recourse must be had to a court. The Houses of Congress are already the judges of the validity and effect of certificates from the components of the electoral college. In that capacity, Congress should, when needful, have those simple powers of a court of equity which would suffice in this situation—the power to reform an instrument to conform to legal obligation, the power to order the execution of an instrument in furtherance of legal obligation, and (overarching both of these remedies) the general equitable power to treat that as done which ought to be done.

None of the foregoing seems to me in the least doubtful, as the law now stands. But it might be as well to codify it all in a revision of title 3, so that it could all roll off automatically if the problem of the "faithless elector" visits us again. The next time, the solution to the problem could determine the identity of the President. Since the people would hardly stand for a person's being President who became President because Congress considered itself impotent to give effect to a plainly implied-in-fact contract, it might be as well to say so at once, in a title 3 revision declaratory of the applicability, to this problem, of simple contract law and remedies. No constitutional amendment would be necessary.

TRENDS IN AMERICAN
CONSTITUTIONAL INTERPRETATION*

Eleven years ago, at about this time in summer, in Providence, Rhode Island, I was in the middle of eight weeks of teaching in a course at Brown University, a course acronymically known as OPAL—The Orientation Program in American Law. The students were lawyers trained in other countries, come to the United States for a year or two of study in our legal system, at one or another of the American law schools. It was thought well—and I think with what proved to be good reason—that they first be given a sort of general view of American legal culture, before going on to Harvard, to Michigan, to Berkeley, to the Southern Methodist University in Dallas, or to many other places—for a more specialized learning. My job was to give them a first look at the American Constitution.

At my opening lecture, I told them that, as travelers in America, they might as well give up on the search, so usual with travelers, for interesting architectural antiquities. "The Texas town I was born in," I told them, "was founded about 1830. There are three buildings on Manhattan Island, the site of New York City, that go back beyond the American Revolution, and none of these goes very far back of that event. The oldest bridge from New York City to Brooklyn was built in 1883, the year of my own father's birth. If, to be sure, you thirst to look on an ancientness beyond mere antiquity, on an ancientness not of

*Prepared for delivery in Ireland in the summer of 1981, in connection with the publication of the O'Reilly and Redmond *Cases and Materials on the Irish Constitution,* the first constitutional law casebook in Ireland. (An accident prevented the trip.)

167

man, go west to the Grand Canyon and the Yellowstone National Park, thousands of miles from here. But as far as old buildings are concerned, we will show you an 'old building' put up in 1845, and those of you who walk to work past the Roman Forum will smile politely behind your hands."

I did not forget, however, to go on to the one human antiquity we do possess. Napoleon Bonaparte, a teen-age second lieutenant, was on leave from his regiment, home in Corsica, in the summer of 1787. Catherine the Great was then on the throne of All the Russias. The Tokugawa Shogunate held Japan aloof from the world. Germany and Italy were geographic expressions.

In that hot Philadelphia summer, a few dozen men got together, and in 100 days wrote the American Constitution; it was speedily ratified, the First Congress assembled; George Washington took the oath of office as President; a Supreme Court was appointed.

Catherine's country then rolled through two hundred years of tyranny and revolution and tyranny again. The country Napoleon soon made his own changed its very basis of legitimacy time after time. Poland disappeared and reappeared. Modern Germany and Italy came to be. Ireland struggled for a long time yet against that simulacrum of a constitution that had been fastened upon her, and at last broke free, after untold wrong and suffering.

And after all these crises, after all these diastrophic, catastrophic motions, that product of 100 days of hard thinking and frank talk, amongst several dozen people in 1787 Philadelphia, is still there, with not so much as a possibly debatable hiatus in the legitimacy of succession. There was a huge partial lapse of authority, in the American Civil War; but that war—the greatest till then, by every measure, in all history—was ended not by a treaty of peace but by a resumption of the general authority of the same government, with several amendments to the same old constitution. All the defeated states sent representatives back to the very same Halls of Congress—"the Houses of their Fathers," as they themselves called them.

"So after all," I told my students, "we do have our one human antiquity—not old at all as buildings go, but rather old as constitutions go. Let us boast not ourselves of tomorrow, for no man knoweth what a day may bring forth, but let us in the meanwhile—in that meanwhile that is all the life there is on earth—give respect and even veneration where these are due."

This meanwhile success of the American Constitution cannot be attributed to the document alone. The text is about 5500 words long, covering some eight or ten pages in big print in an American casebook. To this short text has been addressed one of the most remarkable interpretive efforts in the world's history—possibly the most remarkable such effort ever addressed to a purely secular legal document. It has often been said that the text laid out only a ground-plan, leaving to the future the filling-in of details. But this metaphor falls short of full justice to the facts of the case. It is rather that the text made possible an open series of ground-plans—choice among which had to be made by some other means than merely obeying the directions of the text as given.

It will always be hard to say how much of this work of choice ought to be called "interpretive." With your leave, I will not here essay the sharpening of the suggested distinction. I think that, in a short overview or sampling, the direction of effort toward dealing with these philosophic, psychological and linguistic issues would only get in the way of the beginning of understanding of some of the methods and pressures that have shaped the living American Constitution in the course of its life up to now. Sharp definition along the line between interpretation and new creation, if it ever is to be feasible, will probably have to be accomplished after all the work itself is done—if it ever is done. It is better now to cast out broad lines over an area not exactly bounded. I shall therefore be using both the word and the concept "interpretation" with a looseness that is not meant to resolve these underlying issues of language and of philosophy, but rather to let in all that may be relevant, for whatever it may be worth.

If we look over the whole experience of American constitutional interpretation, some general insights seem to emerge. These insights—or some of them—might perhaps have been guessed at without experience, but to at least one American lawyer they gain a special force from their emerging from interpretive history itself.

The first thing to say is that the whole American experience shows that literalism will not do; the history of American constitutional law and practice can be looked on as a long-continued, a never-ending demonstration of the total insufficiency of literalism. I sometimes start my elementary course in constitutional law by asking the students, "If the Vice-president is impeached by the House of Representatives, and put on trial, on this impeachment, before the Senate, who presides over the trial?" If you were to feed both the Constitution and a good dictionary into a computer, the answer would have to be, "The Vice-president presides over his own trial, unless he is absent from that trial." The Vice-president is to be president of the Senate, unless he is absent. That is what it says in Article I. It isn't as if the framers of the Constitution hadn't thought of the possible unsuitability of the Vice-president as presiding officer over *some* trials of impeachments, because the same Article provides that the Chief Justice shall preside over the trial if the *President* is impeached and put on trial in the Senate.

But of course that won't do. So literalism won't do—at least sometimes. If you think this is a lesson that needs no learning, that is because you have had no occasion to find out how deeply imprinted, in the American layman's picture of legitimate constitutional law method, is the notion that the whole idea, with a written Constitution, is just to do what it says. Part of professionalizing our students is to teach them not to be outraged by the thing that continually happens and very certainly must happen—the seeming message of the constitutional text, considered as a tape fed into a computer, has always been and must continually be molded and modified, supplemented and limited, by techniques very different from the following-out of "meaning" in any simple designative sense. The rationality of American constitutional interpretation has to be the rationality of this set of complexities. It is a rationality partaking of the qualities of art; its abundant copiousness can be illustrated, and particular domains can sometimes be reduced to a satisfying order, but the whole can never be wholly known.

I seem to remember that Carlyle, on being told that a certain lady had decided to accept the universe, exclaimed, "Gad! She'd better." Acceptance of the real universe of American constitutional law can be recommended on grounds perhaps analogous to those that Carlyle had in his mind—only by accepting it can one make anything of it, accomplish anything but chronic discontent with its not being as one had imagined it ought to be.

Yet this acceptance comes hard. Very recently a most eminent American jurist, whom I would blush to identify, announced his adherence to the doctrine that the thing to do with the Constitution was just to read it and do what it says. A great many things might have come in my mind just then; what actually arose was the question, "Well, what about double jeopardy, where imprisonment—maybe twenty years imprisonment—is what is at stake for the defendant?" The Constitution, in its Fifth Amendment, says that no person "shall be subject for the same offense to be twice put in jeopardy *of life or limb* . . ." Nothing about imprisonment. And it isn't as if that subject were just by accident omitted; later on, in the same Amendment, there occurs the famous triad, "life, *liberty* or property," the things of which no one may be deprived "without due process of law." But stay! The plot thickens! Look again. Nothing about "limb," when it comes to not being deprived of one "without due process of law." Yet the word "limb," in another connection, is only fourteen words away from the "due process" clause. Let's ask the computer. Doesn't it print out the judgment that you can be put in jeopardy as many times as it takes to get a conviction, if all that conviction will mean is twenty years for you on the rockpile, but that, on the other hand, as long as you are not put twice in jeopardy, you can be deprived of a limb without due process of law—for all the Constitution has to say about it?

Ridiculous? Exactly. But strong medicine is needed, and no medicine has yet proved wholly efficacious against restrictive literalism. A recent Supreme Court judgment may be chosen from among the many that illustrate this.

The question in the case was whether the Constitution, and in particular its prohibition of "cruel and unusual punishments," forbade certain quite offensive and even disgusting practices in respect of persons who simply awaited trial in jail. Mr. Justice Rehnquist, writing for the Court, triumphantly made the obvious point: "Punishment" is inflicted *after,* not *before,* conviction. These people hadn't been convicted yet; they were just being held for trial. How could it be said that what was being done to them was "punishment"? And if it wasn't "punishment," how could it be "cruel and unusual punishment"?

That sounds fine, until one goes back and notes that the same style of reasoning would make it all right to put people twice in jeopardy of imprisonment for the same offense, or to deprive a person of a limb without due process of law.

Literalism, in my observation, is always highly selective. A benign case is that of Mr. Justice Hugo Black's insistence that the constitutional guarantee of freedom of speech and of the press was an "absolute," admitting no exceptions. He stressed herein the phrase ". . . *no law* abridging freedom of speech or of the press. . . ." He stuck to this absolutist position through thick and thin. Yet this noble pertinacity—and in dark days it was surely noble—concealed fundamental difficulties. An accidental but impressive one was that Senator Hugo Black of Alabama had been the principal author and sponsor of the highly significant Securities and Exchange Act, which was a vast and stringent set of restrictions on what you could say, or print, to promote the sale of stocks and bonds. This opens the tent-flap to a rather large camel of doubt: Can Justice Black really have thought through the false advertising question, the incitement-to-murder question? Had he considered that the full phrase, from which he extracted the phrase "no law," was "*Congress* shall make no law"? What about police actions in Birmingham, Alabama? On the other hand, Mr. Justice Black, at one period, judged that the First Amendment guarantees extended to picketing in labor disputes. Yet, from a literal standpoint, such picketing need involve neither "speech" nor "press," in any but an extended metaphorical sense that quite dissolves the whole literalist enterprise.

In a way, the inevitable end of the road came when Mr. Justice Black insisted that when black youths stood peacefully in a public library, protesting their exclusion, this action was unprotected by the "free speech" guarantee, because it was not "speech."

In a talk of anything like tolerable length, I can do no more than suggest a few insights into our American experience. The insight I am suggesting here is that a severe literalism in the application of constitutional guarantees is incompatible with the existence of a systematic equity, as rational as it can be made, of such guarantees. This is not to say that such literalism is wrong. It is to face forthrightly the terrible price one pays for it. Facing that price, one must be motivated to find an honest technical and professional way out of it. We are now, in America, very much in midstream on this. What we have done and may be doing cannot be presented as a work finished; it is a work in progress. I shall return to this theme after a little while. Just now I want to fill in on a very few other major interpretive issues.

A general point I want to fill in now is of absolutely cardinal importance. This is that American judicial review for constitu-

tionality—as, indeed, all interpretive work on our Constitution—takes place in and with regard to our *federal* system. Our
system has been classically conceived as one in which the central
government is of limited powers, while the state governments
possess full residual powers, except for the impact of particular
national laws and specific constitutional provisions. Anyone
who saw the power relations in our federalism as practically
conforming to this pattern would be in for some disappoint-
ments. In fact and truth, we have a national government which
is the next thing to *generally* empowered, and state governments
restricted not only by particular and specific constitutional and
statutory provisions but also by limiting doctrines of considerable generality. Obviously, we got there by interpretation, at
least in the loose sense in which I am using that word.

Let me take just the matter of the affirmative scope of the
national powers—the construction associated with the name of
our great Chief Justice John Marshall.

Marshall's doctrines were nationalist all the way, and this
shows up even in some relatively narrow solutions of little if
any more than lexicographic scale. For example, it was one of
the holdings of the early case of *Gibbons v. Ogden,* that the word
"commerce" included "navigation," so that the national congressional power to regulate "commerce with foreign nations
and among the several states" includes the power to regulate
navigation on the public waters of the United States.

But there are far more general themes in the interpretive
work on national power. These may be suggested by three questions: First, what scope of choice is there for selection of *means*
of employing one or more of the national powers? Secondly,
what *ends* may be sought by the employment of the national
powers? Thirdly, what kind of connection must there be between
a train of events and a named national power, for that power to
be exercisable over that train of events?

Marshall, in the great opinion in *McCulloch v. Maryland,*
dealt with the first of these questions so thoroughly as to make

all that came after a mere mopping-up operation. The question was whether Congress might validly create the Bank of the United States, a nationally chartered corporation. The objection was that the Constitution named no power to form a bank, or to charter any corporation. Marshall's answer was that the facilities of fund-transfer, credit management, and all the other facilities offered by a national bank, were *means* adapted to the efficient execution of certain of Congress' named powers, and that the power to do a thing included necessarily the power to find and choose among the means of doing it. To the objection that Congress was not empowered to form a corporation and endow it with corporate life, much the same answer was given; a corporation, said Marshall, is never set up for itself, but always as an *instrument* for attaining some end; the incorporated Bank of the United States was a means toward executing Congress' powers. These doctrines, once established, remained in place, and in one sense they form the bed-rock foundation of the United States Government as it actually exists. Because of course what was said of banks and corporations had a wider application than to just those entities.

On the second question, the movement was slower. But the earliest attempts by Congress to use its powers for ends not themselves suggested by the nature of the powers were all upheld. The most fateful case was probably Champion v. Ames, decided in 1904. Congress had forbidden the interstate shipment of lottery tickets—with the undisguised purpose of suppressing lotteries. In a 5-4 decision, the Supreme Court upheld this act. The statute was very plainly and literally a "regulation of commerce among the several states." The motive of such regulation, the Court majority said, was immaterial. The case was soon followed by a number of others, using both the national commercial power and the national taxing power in such ways as to promote some activities, and discourage or forbid others.

In the famous case of *Hammer v. Dagenhart,* decided in 1918, a majority of the Court, perceiving the enormous strategic importance of this line of interpretation, gave the process momentary check by striking down an Act of Congress prohibiting the interstate shipment of goods manufactured by child labor. But by this time Mr. Justice Holmes, in his great dissent, was able to show that the Court's judgment had no ancestry in any precedents, but instead contradicted the uniform line of authority up to the time. The case had no future either; almost immediately decisions began coming down that were in fact quite irreconcilable with it. It was formally overruled in 1941, but both before and since that overruling a torrent of cases has established, over an enormous range, the principle that Congress may use its powers for any end not actually forbidden—as, for example, the guarantee of a free press would forbid a law making it a crime to carry a Socialist newspaper across a state line.

The third question—what causal or other connection must there be between regulated conduct and events open to Congressional regulation—went through a similar development. In 1871, in *The Daniel Ball,* it was held that national safety regulations might constitutionally apply to a steamer on which were carried goods that were to move in interstate commerce, although the steamer itself never crossed a state line. At the farther end of a long procession of cases, covering a wide factual range, stands the 1946 case of *Wickard v. Filburn,* holding that the national Department of Agriculture may constitutionally be empowered to regulate the growth of wheat on one's own farm, for consumption there, on the ground that, in the national aggregate, these actions affect the interstate and foreign market in wheat.

Now that's a long way from the concept of central government of limited powers, with the states mostly running their own concerns. And, while I have chosen to confine the field of examples to uses of the commerce clause, a very closely parallel development has taken place as to the taxing power, and virtually all the enumerated national powers are at one time or another used in this way—the spending power by no means least, in either volume or importance. In consequence of all these things, we have a fully national government.

Now as a sheer intellectual matter, you can think what you like about the trends of interpretation that have led us to this place. From this point of view alone, I think well of them. I started by smiling at *Wickard v. Filburn,* the homegrown wheat case. I stopped smiling when I informed myself enough about the matter to be sure that the growing and consumption of wheat at home does, in fact and truth, palpably affect the interstate wheat market. But what I want to use all this for at this time is to illustrate—as it can be made very powerfully to illustrate—the placement of constitutional interpretation in the political process.

All these cases, from the Bank of the United States case to the home-grown wheat case, have all too often been presented (and not only in the press, where one expects such things) as though what were involved were rather aggressive acts of judicial interpretation, expanding the national power by merest judicial motion. There could be no plainer an error. In every single case, without any possible exception in the very nature of things, the initial act of expansive interpretation must have been made *by the Congress*—either with formal presidential approval or by the heavy majorities, in both Houses of Congress, necessary to override a presidential veto. The Supreme Court's actions are—as they can only be—ratificatory of action already taken. To generalize this point, the finally decisive expansion of the federal power into true national power has been a work—of interpretation and of will—performed by the nation itself, acting through its authorized political organs. This may be obvious enough to you, as you look at the matter freshly. It is not so obvious in the United States, where the self-evidently false myth of the Supreme Court as the aggressor seems to be inexpugnably dug in.

And the point goes a little further. The opposition, in all

these cases, is between national and state power. And here we have to do with another myth—the myth of the national government as a sort of hostile occupying power. In fact, the very same people live in the nation and in the states; the same people send representatives to Congress and to the state legislatures. The assent to any Act of Congress is an assent by representatives of the people of the states.

There is another important political consideration, bearing on the phase of interpretation wherein the judicial branch does become implicated, at least as ratifier and legitimater of a use of national power. Let me illustrate. In the Lottery Ticket case, fateful as it was for federalism, a man was punished for shipping lottery tickets from California to Texas. His claim of immunity rested on the contention that the statute hindered and hampered the conduct of lotteries in either Texas or California or both, and that the proper determiners of policy toward lotteries were these states—that the Act of Congress "invaded the powers of the states" over this local subject. *But there was no showing of any objection on the part of either Texas or California.* This is far more often than not the case; the claimant of immunity on a "states-rights" ground is claiming on the basis of the rights of a polity that may be in no way aggrieved.

And let me touch on yet another point I believe to be significant enough to have explained, without more, the air of inevitability in this development. Let me put the matter this way: One person may think ill of the regulation of homegrown wheat. Another may think the Stolen Automobiles Act a little too much. Another may deplore the national narcotic regulation activities. And so on. But as time has gone on, and these powers have snowballed and become visible in their generality, there is hardly any interest-group left that does not, above all, want to harness a little of this power to its own use. The result is that *really principled* "strict constructionism" has little or no constituency.

Far, then, from being the aggressor, the judicial branch, in all these cases through a century and three-quarters, is only *declining to interfere* with the exercise of national powers claimed by the political branches. It is declining to interfere in the interest of states whose posture on the matter is usually not known. It is declining to interfere on the basis of doctrines which have virtually no really principled constituency. And at the end of the day the whole sinister result is that the United States, like most other nations, has a national government after all—as far as its people, speaking through Congress, want one. I'm glad I like this result, because I don't see how it could have been prevented, so narrowly was the process channelled by the political factors I have mentioned.

Now let me move back to the problem I let stand a little while ago—the problem of building a regime, a *system* of human rights, as part of our Constitution. A narrow literalism will not do this, almost or perhaps entirely in the very nature of things. There is more to this than the howling absurdities I started with. Beyond all that, it is most unlikely that the makers and amenders of any constitution will have the prophetic gift, in both senses of that adjective, needful for constructing a comprehensive working system of this sort, in the kind of fine grain that would ensure a satisfactory result by the mere clarity of reference in the language.

As with all our American works of constitutional interpretation, this problem is set, for us, in the framework of federalism. Before I explain the technics of this, I should like to mention a large and I think interesting fact about the impact of our "Bill of Rights" material—as we often call, collectively, those parts of our Constitution guaranteeing human rights against government invasion. I refer to the fact that, in overwhelmingly dominant proportion, judicial application of this "Bill of Rights" material is to *actions of the states*. This fact surprises some people at home, because we usually start our students off, in constitutional law, with a case called *Marbury v. Madison,* wherein Mr. Chief Justice Marshall confirmed the duty and the power of the courts, with the Supreme Court at the top, to treat as nullities those Acts of the national Congress which were thought by the courts to violate the Constitution. The reasoning—even the political philosophy—of that case is treated with the most tender and lengthy care. And the case does indeed state an interesting doctrine. But the fact is that, through all the past and to a most decided degree in the last forty years, judicial invalidations of governmental action, on the ground of its violating human-rights guarantees in the federal constitution, have been directed principally against actions of the *states* or of *state* officials. There is no problem of any kind about the legitimacy of this kind of "declaration of unconstitutionality." The reasonings of *Marbury v. Madison* play no part; the matter is thoroughly covered, and put entirely out of doubt, by the language of the national Constitution and of Acts of Congress conferring jurisdiction on the federal courts.

I think these facts very importantly—and quite legitimately—condition the attitudes of the courts in this branch of their work of constitutional interpretation. It must be, first, that *national* material of a most solemn kind will tend to be given a large and liberal interpretation vis-à-vis the actions of the lesser included authority.

Special factors may for a time have impeded the development suggested by this thought. Here I must offer a technical explanation. Before the American Civil War, and indeed until around 1868, there was nothing like general federal protection of human rights out in the states; the national Bill of Rights proper—the first eight amendments—had been firmly held not to apply to the states at all. There remained only a few rather narrow protective provisions, expressly directed against the states, in the Constitution proper. These were important in a way, because their application by the courts established the habit of this way of work, and may somehow subliminally have implanted the idea that the judicially enforced constitutional limitation of state activity, in the interest of national ideas about justice, was a con-

genital feature of the Republic. But the visibility of these
provisions, and their influence on life, were by several orders of
magnitude less than the corresponding things became in consequence of the adoption of the Fourteenth Amendment, as part
of the winding-up of the Civil War. It will save words in the
long run for me to read you out the fateful Section 1 of that
Amendment:

> All persons born or naturalized in the United States, and sub-
> ject to the jurisdiction thereof, are citizens of the United States
> and of the State wherein they reside. No State shall make or enforce
> any law which shall abridge the privileges or immunities of citizens
> of the United States; nor shall any State deprive any person of life,
> liberty, or property, without due process of law; nor deny to any
> person within its jurisdiction the equal protection of the laws.

Now here we are not dealing anymore with a few narrow
exceptions to the general rule of plenary state governmental
power, but with broad general principles.

Yet for a long time these provisions virtually slept, except
for application to economic and business activity, a field wherein
they might have been thought least likely to succeed. I think
one reason for this was that, if they were to apply to human
rights at all, the obvious and central place for their application,
in view of their placement in history, was in the field of race and
racism, and the country had come to the hardly so much as tacit
understanding that nothing much was to be done, in the fore-
seeable future, for the blacks of America. The striking-down of
wages and hours laws, on the ground of their interference with
freedom of contract, was easy to keep separate from racist
oppression. It would not have been so easy to maintain this
separation in the presence of a spacious and generalized development regarding the privileges and immunities of citizenship,
a human status. This is only a guess; perhaps deeper than that
was a general lack of moral energy, for a long time.

But at around the time of the Brown case—striking down

the segregation system and so announcing that the anti-racist component of the Fourteenth Amendment was to be taken seriously and acted upon—pressure seems to have begun to mount for a *general systematic equity* of human rights, based, as against action of the states, on the Fourteenth Amendment's general words.

From this point on, what we have to do with is a very curious development in legal artifacts, a development at the roots and reasons of which one can only guess. There were several themes.

First (with a few early antecedents, quite irregular in their own time) the due process clause of the Fourteenth Amendment came to be seen as embodying or expressing certain substantive guarantees. The national protection of freedom of speech against state action, which was not finally accepted in the Supreme Court till 1925, was an offshoot of this process. More generally, the phrase "substantive due process" came to be heard, and is still heard. I tell my students, when we get to that part of the book, that they ought to stand in front of a mirror every morning and evening, and several times pronounce the phrase "*substantive due process*" "Substantive due *what*?" "*What* due process." I think of the phrase as a Zen Buddhist Koan, apt to emancipate the soul through the chain-breaking force of iron-willed persistence in paradox, but not as encapsulating very much explanatory power. Try it sometime.

Meanwhile, what we call the "incorporation" controversy marched on. To what extent, if at all, did the Fourteenth Amendment "incorporate" the old Bill of Rights proper? I am a man of mercy, and I will spare you the details of that ancient controversy. In the end, for all practical purposes, and without regard to the choicer precisions of theory, the Supreme Court seems to have settled down on the idea that the "due process" part of the Fourteenth Amendment "incorporates" at least the important parts of the old Bill of Rights proper—freedom of petition, right to counsel, and so on. Like Hugo Black, I should have thought that the "privileges and immunities" clause of the Fourteenth Amendment was a better "incorporation" vehicle but, like him, I am willing to settle and everybody—with one always possible exception, has seemed to settle on "incorporation" of at least the more important parts of the old Bill of Rights in the Fourteenth Amendment, and so on their being applicable against the states.

So let's start reading in the Bill of Rights. We soon get to the part, in the Eighth Amendment, about the cruel and unusual punishments; it's all pretty short. Might as well finish . . . what's this?

AMENDMENT IX

The enumeration in the Constitution, of certain rights, shall not be construed to deny or disparage others retained by the people.

Were we talking about a quest for the technical foundation of a general and developing systematic equity of human rights?

Well, an eminent Irish judge, in a judgment I read in the excellent book we are today launching on what I am sure will be a distinguished and seminal career, looked across the Ocean Sea, saw the Ninth Amendment, and assumed, as one would think any intelligent lawyer would, that we have here all we need as a foundation for the most gloriously towering cathedral of human rights law, stone placed on carefully cut stone. Of course he was right about the Ninth Amendment. Perhaps he should brush up a bit on the capacity of Americans for not seeing or hearing what is so clearly presented. (We used to recite, in the primary school I attended in Austin, Texas, a Pledge of Allegiance that spoke of "One nation indivisible, with liberty and justice for all." [The part about "God" was put in later, in the pietistic days of Eisenhower.] The black children of Austin, for all I know, may have been reciting the same words, in their own school out back o'town.)

The Ninth Amendment used rarely to be mentioned. It has

never been the actual foundation of any judicial judgment in the United States. That is the staggering fact.

That is why, in my Holmes Lectures at Harvard last year, I thought it well to move that the Ninth Amendment to the Constitution of the United States, having been duly proposed and ratified, be now adopted.

What would we get from it? Well, we are instructed by it, first, that unnamed rights are not to be denied or disparaged. I infer from that that we are being told they are to be taken to exist in American constitutional law. What then? Well, we can just declare their existence, put up a commemorative cairn, and forget all about the matter, or we can *try to find them,* by such methods as we have—by analogic reasoning from rights already known, by the best reasoning we can bring to the structures and relationships of our polity, by inference from the concept of citizenship. We'll never be quite sure we are right in every such step taken. But are we ever quite sure, anywhere, in law?

For years and years, we didn't see the Ninth Amendment because we were running away from it. Maybe we were right; maybe the Ninth Amendment was really too much for us, just for then. Maybe we needed first to get a little further along with such special matters as equality for blacks, freedom of expression, minimal fairness in criminal trials. The work of interpretation has its historical pace. But we have stopped running, and seem to be looking about us now for some technically acceptable basis for the systematic generalization of human rights. Some of us have turned all the way about, seen the Ninth Amendment, and begun walking toward the ground it has occupied and prepared. It is not too soon for us to be doing that. But it is not too late either.

I've tried my best to take you through the broadest outlines of our two greatest interpretive enterprises.

The one created the national government of the United States as it is. With all else there is to recommend that process as we look back on it and look now on its results, its best recommendation is that, without it, the government of the United States would have been born dead. The avoidance of that result is the first commandment of constitutional interpretation.

The other process is only just well begun. I like to think, even on other days than patriotic holidays, that the ultimate purpose of the first process was that it enabled us to turn our attention to the second. On this second one, because it is only well begun, the realistic presentation has had to be of a process in being, with all the doubt and even controversiality that that implies.

We have an old Constitution, but we are a young nation, much younger than you. Wish us well as our work of interpretation proceeds—as we wish you well, and your marvellous new book—and its authors. May your work of interpretation, and ours, be blessed!

ON READING AND USING
THE NINTH AMENDMENT*

For the reader's convenience, I will set out the brief text of the Ninth Amendment to the Constitution of the United States:

> The enumeration in the Constitution, of certain rights, shall not be construed to deny or disparage others retained by the people.

This sentence stands at the end of a very short "enumeration" of rights—an "enumeration" nobody could possibly think anywhere near sufficient for guarding even the values it patchily and partially shields. The Ninth Amendment language was put where it is by people who believed they were enacting for an indefinite future. All sorts of other language may have been used around this language. But this was the language chosen to become "valid to all Intents and Purposes, as Part of [the] Constitution. . . ." What does it seem to be saying?

It could be read as saying that nobody really ought to deny, in discourse of a mixed moral and political tenor, that a number of rights exist, beyond the enumerated ones. But this is quite unbelievable. Virtually all of the Constitution, including the amendments preceding and later following this one, is *law*, sparely stated in the language of law. Attention here should be focused especially on the first eight amendments, together with which the Ninth Amendment entered the Constitution. These are austere, peremptory directions to law-making and law-en-

---

*Originally published in a *Festschrift* volume tendered to Eugene V. Rostow, *Power and Policy in Quest of Law.* Dordrecht: Martinus Nijhoff, 1985.

forcing officials, from Congress, through courts of law, down to magistrates issuing search warrants and military officers quartering troops. In the Constitution as a whole, and in this immediate context, the insertion of a precept of moral philosophy would not merely have changed the subject abruptly, but would have put the content of this Amendment in quite a different world from that of the Constitution, and of the "enumerated" rights just set out.

The Amendment could be read as saying no more than that the bare fact of "enumeration" of other rights should not, in and of itself, give rise to the inference that no other rights exist, but that the forbidding of the drawing of this one inference in no way prejudices the question whether there really are, in addition to the enumerated rights, any "others retained by the people." I guess a computer, fed the words, would have to print this out as a logical possibility. I submit that it is not a serious psychological possibility that anyone totally neutral on the question of the existence of rights not "enumerated" would bother to set up this kind of directive as to what course the non-logic of *expressio unius* may take, leaving it quite open that the very same conclusion—no non-enumerated rights—may be reached by some other path of reasoning. The Ninth Amendment seems to be guarding something; such bother is not likely to be taken if the question is thought to be quite at large whether there is anything out there to be guarded.

It should be noted, in passing, that the most one could get out of even this computer-print is that the language of the Ninth Amendment does not *affirmatively imply* the existence of unenumerated rights; even a computer would have to print out that this language implies that such rights *may* exist—if you also fed into that computer the assumption: "The utterers of this language were not talking just to hear their heads rattle." This, while not strictly an existence-proof, would be a proof of the serious possibility of the existence of rights not enumerated; even this might be enough to legitimate a further quest. But the

Constitution is not a computer-program, and I submit that preponderance of reason leaves us with the conclusion, about as well supported as any we can reach in law, that the Ninth Amendment declares as a matter of law—of constitutional law, overriding other law—that some other rights are "retained by the people," and that these shall be treated as *on an equal footing* with rights enumerated.

This would have to mean that these rights "not enumerated" may serve as the substantive basis for judicial review of governmental actions; any other conclusion would not only do violence to expectations naturally shaped by the command that these other rights not be "denied or disparaged" in respect to the enumerated rights, but would also lead one back around to the inadmissible idea, discussed above, that this Amendment, placed where it is, is merely a directive for the course of moral philosophy or of purely political argument. Nor does it make any difference whether the possibility of judicial review was immediately present to everyone's mind at just the moment the Ninth Amendment passed Congress, or was ratified by the last necessary state. The idea that constitutional rights were to form the substantive basis of such review was so much in the air (and in the laws) that it is unlikely it was overlooked by the *major et sanior pars*. But in any case the direction of the Ninth Amendment—that non-enumerated rights not be "denied or disparaged," as against enumerated rights—was directed literally at the future, at the corpus of law-to-be, and affirmative settlement of the question (if, as I doubt, it was a real question in 1790) of the rightness of judicial review, on the basis of *any* right "enumerated" in the Constitution, would settle the rightness of judicial review on the basis of those rights not enumerated, though "retained by the people," because anything else would "deny or disparage" these latter, in a quite efficacious way.

The only hitch is, in short, that the rights not enumerated are not enumerated. We are not told what they are. So the question is, "What do you do when you are solemnly told, by an authority to which you owe fidelity, to protect a designated set of things in a certain way, but are, in the very nature of the case, not told what particular things this set comprises?"

There are two possible courses to follow. One is to throw up your hands and say that no action is possible, because you haven't been told exactly how to act. The other is to take the Ninth Amendment as a command to use any rational methods available to the art of law, and with these in hand to set out to discover what it is you are to protect.

The first of these leads right back around, yet again, to a *practical* "denial and disparagement" of the rights not enumerated; it leads, indeed, to something a shade more imbecile than taking the Amendment as a direction of the course of moral philosophy, for it disclaims any power even to discover what rights are not to be "denied or disparaged" in out-of-court discourse. But at least you stay out of trouble.

The second course gets you into deep troubles. First is the trouble of deciding, by preponderance of reason, what *methods* are to be seen as legitimate, in our legal culture, for making out the shape of the rights not named. Then there is the trouble—since no known legal method produces anything like certain results—of deciding where the preponderance of reason lies on the merits of *any particular claim of right,* when that claim is weighed by the methods you have decided are legitimate. And the worst of it is that these troubles will never be done with, or even lessened. The methods of law are not a closed canon. The problems they must solve are infinite and unforeseeable. The solutions will never have the quality of the Pythagorean Theorem; time may even bring the conviction that some solutions, though confidently arrived at, were wrong, and must be revised.

Altogether, it's a lot of troubles. Maybe we ought to give up, and let the Ninth Amendment—and the priceless rights it refers to—keep gathering dust for a third century.

But there is one thing to note about the very real troubles that face us when we turn to the search that the Ninth Amendment seems to command. *These are the troubles not of the Ninth Amendment itself, but of law.* If they put one off the Ninth Amendment enterprise, maybe one ought to give up law altogether, try something else. But that course has its own problems. To turn to medicine, to music, to history—even to mathematical physics—is to accept the burden of troubles rather closely analogous to those of Ninth Amendment law, or of law as a whole. For my part, too old to train for anything else, I would accept the challenge of Ninth Amendment law, as the same old (and forever new) challenge of law. (I shall explain, below, my use of the terms "Ninth Amendment law" and "Ninth Amendment right.")

What methods are legitimate for finding and giving shape to the non-enumerated rights guarded by the Ninth Amendment?

Let me start with a rejection. Some people, faced with this question, would try to dig up every scrap of paper that happens to have survived since the eighteenth century, and to piece together some sort of "intent," with very little weight given to the transcendently relevant piece of paper, the one on which the duly enacted text of the Ninth Amendment was written.

I am one who thinks that, in a general way, our legal culture carries this sort of thing much too far. We sometimes treat statements made informally in one House of Congress as the exact equivalent, in everything but name, of formal statutory language; if it is right to do that, what are the formalities for? In the very teeth of Madison's quite sound and reiterated insistence that the records of the 1787 Constitution, not being publicly known until decades after the government was formed, ought not to be used to establish the public meaning of the Constitution's text, we sometimes seem to treat these records as all but superior in authority to that text itself. If we had to choose between our style of getting drunk on collateral and sometimes casual evidences of "intent," and leaving the stuff altogether alone, as the British do, I would choose the latter course—

though I think sometimes a very cautious use of such material may be warranted.

But if there ever was a case where informal collateral evidence of "intent" must be useless, it is in regard to the finding of the rights that belong in the class of "others retained by the people." This language of the Ninth Amendment is apt for referring to things you haven't thought of or quite agreed upon; such language would be hopelessly inapt as a sort of coded-message reference to a closed class of "rights" you *have* thought of and agreed upon. If the decoded message read that rights A, B, C, D, *and no others*, were not to be "denied or disparaged," then the peculiar result would have been reached that we would have two kinds of "enumeration," the second kind being a coded enumeration, and that these *two* kinds of "enumeration" exhausted the class of rights to be protected, so that other rights, not thus "enumerated" *could* be "denied or disparaged." The informally arrived-at "enumeration" would thus be given an "*expressio unius*" force explicitly denied to the formal "enumeration" elsewhere. Something would have gone wrong here; doubtless the Greeks had a word for that kind of paradox. I am content to say that it seems to me to have no place in the robust common-sense world of the best work on American constitutional law.

If, on the other hand, the decoded message of the Ninth Amendment turned out to be that rights A, B, C, and D are not to be denied or disparaged, but that this class is *not* closed, then we are right where we were, with (in effect) *another* amendment "enumerating" rights A, B, C, and D, and a Ninth Amendment still commanding that rights not "enumerated" shall not be denied or disparaged.

Some pause might be given if we found a real consensus, uniting the *major pars* of the relevant eighteenth-century people, that some identifiable claim to a "right" was *not* to be looked on as guarded by the Ninth Amendment. But this would be a pause only. "Due process" is an evolving concept; "cruel and unusual punishment" is an evolving concept; the language of the Ninth Amendment seems even more apt than these to be mentioning an evolving set of rights, not to be bounded even by a negative eighteenth-century judgment based on eighteenth-century evaluations and social facts as then seen. And one would have to remember that even the arbitrary blackballing of one "right" or several "rights," on the basis of "intent" evidence, would in no way impair the generality of the Ninth Amendment's command as to the other rights not enumerated.

I have treated this issue of collaterally evidenced "intent" quite abstractly; I don't know of any corpus of actual evidence that would enable or oblige one to treat it more concretely.

To me, the upshot is that we have to take this language as it comes to us. We are its inheritors; it "belongs in usufruct to the living," as Jefferson said of the earth. If we regard it (as I do) as directing us to do our best to discover for ourselves what enumerated rights are to be given sanction, so that we may obey the Ninth Amendment command against their denial or disparagement, there is really no dearth of sound and well-tested methods for obeying this command, and so moving in the direction of a rational and coherent corpus juris of human rights.

This statement gains a great deal of plausibility, or more, from the fact that we have for a very long time been protecting unnamed rights. We have done this, sometimes, under the guise of treating the language of the Constitution as highly metaphoric or otherwise figurative, as when we see "speech" or "press" in picketing and black armbands, or see the making of a noise near someone's land as a "taking." But the *appropriateness* of any such metaphoric extension can be explored only by asking, for example, "Is the wearing of a black armband so similar, in relevant respects, to speech, that it ought to be treated as speech is treated?" And when we ask this question we recognize an old friend—the common law method of arguing from the established to the not yet established, weighing similarities and differences, and deciding where the balance lies. Sometimes, as in the common law, this method creates a whole new heading, as with the "freedom of association" now generally recognized as arising, by the discernment of functional equivalence or analogy, from the First Amendment rights literally "enumerated." This is how (for one example more) we achieved the result of applying the double jeopardy clause to cases where *imprisonment* is the penalty, though, if you read the Fifth Amendment, you find that, as named or "enumerated," this protection applies only to "jeopardy of life or limb." If, in time of peace, government attempted the "quartering" of sailors or government civilian employees in houses without the consent of the owners, or if consent was had from the "owner" of an apartment house but not from a tenant in possession under a lease, rational legal discourse could be addressed to the questions all these actions would raise in confrontation with the Third Amendment. You could, of course, talk as though the questions were whether a sailor is "really" a soldier, whether the tenant of an apartment is "really" the owner of a house—but even in this disguise these questions could be rationally addressed only by adding to them the phrase "in preponderantly relevant respects," or some such language. And this would lead right into the eternal question, "Is this a difference that *ought to make a difference?*" This question sounds familiar, because it is, first, a question repeated infinite times in the quest for rational justice, and, secondly, because it is the question continually asked—and answered in each case as best it may be—by the common law, the matrix of all our particular legal methodology. The issue is not whether the use of this method would be a bizarre innovation; the issue is whether any quest for decent law, with its parts rationally related, can possibly do without it.

Nor need this method of "analogy" be used only for small motions, like the supplying of the hiatus in the double jeopardy clause. The seeking of consistent rationality is a requirement of all good law, at every level of generality. If the central meaning of the equal protection clause is—as it surely is—the forbidding of discrimination against *blacks,* then the propriety of applying that clause to discrimination against *women* can be reasoned about by marshalling the similarities (the genetic and indelible character of the trait, the maintenance of the discriminatory regime by social stereotypes, and so on) in confrontation with the differences (for example, absence of whole-family discrimination stretching back through history). And, since this is both a real and a complicated case, the Nineteenth Amendment would also serve as a starting-point for the eternal similarity-difference reasoning of law questing for justice: If women may not be excluded from voting, may they be excluded from office-holding? From jury service? And so on.

I must resist the impulse toward—and am really glad to eschew—any attempt here and now to build a corpus juris of human rights on this basis, or on the others to be mentioned below. In a proper and profound sense, that corpus will never be built; it will always be building, like the common law. If this method is not rational, then neither is the common law. And neither is any other attempt to give due effect to similarities and differences between already decided and newly presented cases and problems.

There is another generative principle in our legal system, the principle that law may be generated by due attention to the sound requirements arising out of social or political structures and relations. This is how we got the warranty of fitness for human consumption in the sale of food; this is also how, in some states, we have recently gotten that warranty extended to bind the manufacturer and packager or canner, when structures and relationships changed in the food trade. This is how we got the insurers' right of subrogation, and the testimonial privilege for communications between penitent and priest. This is how we got the obligation of parents to care for their children. Our law—and, I venture to say, *all* law—has been and is continually being shaped and reshaped by this generative principle. It is the principle from which we first derived the right—not literally "enumerated"—to move from one state to another.

Now if we had only these two master methods—the method of similarity-difference reasoning from the committed to the not yet committed, and the method of reasoning from structures and relationships—we would have the means of building toward a rationally consistent, comprehensive and fairly serviceable law of human rights. There is no question here of discerning that these rights are in any designative sense "mentioned" or "incorporated" in the Ninth Amendment, or that they derive from that Amendment; the language of the Amendment suggests—or commands, as I think—a question outside itself, a quest for rights *nowhere* enumerated, not the mere tracing out of its references, which are purposefully of total vagueness.

But methods, in any mature and subtle legal culture, are never a closed class. Law ought to be seen to contain not only the means of striving toward rational consistency, not only the means of keeping the rules of legal decision in tune with the society's structures and relationships, but also the means—the methods—for reaching toward higher goals. Herein is the very best of what was so beautifully called, by Lon Fuller, "The Law in Quest of Itself." With the carefulness that is a condition of law's rationality, we may be able to discern and validate "other rights retained by the people" as latent in, and therefore susceptible of being drawn from, the noblest of concepts to which our nation is committed.

The two best sources for such concepts are the Declaration of Independence and the Preamble to the Constitution. To illustrate, I will take the concept that is common to these, the concept of "liberty." If we are committed to anything, it is to the idea of "liberty." If that commitment doesn't really refer to anything except a good inner feeling, we ought to shut up about it.

There is of course an enormous area wherein the concept or idea of "liberty" solves no problems. But it would be very careless to conclude from this that the concept has no problem-solving power at all, no power to generate "unenumerated rights" by rational operations. "Loyalty to one's friends" and "kindness to one's children" are quite vague in some ranges. But we cannot and do not conclude from this that we can never identify actions, and broad classes of actions, which constitute disloyalty to one's friends, or unkindness to one's children. If concepts like these were really totally vague, through their entire range, society would fall to pieces—or, rather, would never have formed itself. A serious dedication to "liberty" seems to resemble these other concepts in that, while it is vague in much of its range, we can still identify some things that are inconsistent with this serious dedication to "liberty."

It seems to me that a serious *and thoroughly general* commitment to liberty is inconsistent with restrictions or deprivations grossly out of proportion, in their impact on persons, to the benefits that may reasonably be anticipated by the society that imposes them. Every term in this formula is vague in a good part of its range. But, again, there is likely to be no difficulty in identifying at least some instances in which most people would agree that the gross disproportion is visible—sometimes even grotesque. If this is so, then at least some "unenumerated" rights may be generated by the proportionality principle, and so pass into the corpus juris of human rights.

Indeed, this principle seems supported even by the kind of analogic reasoning discussed above, for the idea of proportionality is seen several times in the first eight amendments: "*excessive* bail," "*excessive* fines," "*unreasonable* searches and seizures." The idea of proportionality is just below the surface at other points; it is a part, for example, of the now-accepted definition of "cruel and unusual punishment." In absolute terms, this is not much—but it is quite a lot in a Bill of Rights of some 500 words in all.

The actual judgment of gross disproportionality must be made case by case and field by field; that is in the very nature of the test itself. And in this area, perhaps more than in most others, continual shifting and readjustments, at the borderland, would be bound to occur, because knowledge and insight, both as to the harshness of impact on individuals and as to the benefit reasonably to be anticipated by society, must change from time to time.

This proportionality standard would none the less have power. It could, for example, easily explain the judgment, controversial in its own time, that nullified state anti-contraceptive laws; the state that came to bar in that case scarcely made a serious effort to establish any very likely or very large beneficial effect of the prohibition it had imposed, as weighed against the crushing effect the statute would have, if enforced, on the personal lives of citizens. Many past decisions, looked on as highly problematic in their days, would easily yield to justification on proportionality grounds, and such grounds are in fact very near the surface—sometimes virtually explicit—in a good range of such cases.

"Liberty," with the "proportionality" rule it seems to me to generate, is only one instance of such a well-authenticated and generative value. The "pursuit of happiness" as an "inalienable right," the promotion "of the general welfare" and the establishment of "justice" as goals of our political association—these may assert their power in time. Even the dogmata of the Catholic Church have unfolded gradually; we can scarcely expect any more of our constitutional law—and the history of that law amply shows that it is utterly idle to think all questions can be answered at once. We may come to see, for example, that the *effective* "pursuit of happiness" is not really possible to those hobbled and hamstrung by physical and intellectual malnutrition in childhood, and in young adulthood doomed to exclusion from rewarding or even remunerative work, through no fault of their own.

It is time to sum up what I have tried to say.

Of course, no "rights" are "Ninth Amendment rights," in the sense of their being simply referred to or "incorporated" in the general language of that Amendment, and so deriving both their shape and their positive force from it. On overwhelming preponderance of reason, it seems to me, the Amendment *recognizes the existence* of such rights, and, by its command that they not be denied or disparaged, commands in the same breath (as the command of the end commands the means) that they be sought for and given shape by use of whatever rational means may be available within our legal culture—because the abstention from this search and shaping would be the most efficacious possible denial and disparagement. (When I say, anywhere, "Ninth Amendment rights," or "Ninth Amendment law," I mean to symbolize this relation.)

We possess powerful tools for this work. We can reason from analogy, functional similarity, common underlying values, and the like, using "enumerated" rights as points of departure. We can shape rules that arise out of the structures and relationships of our society—our political society chiefly, but not necessarily that society alone. As to both these methods, they are of a rationality and utility demonstrated beyond a doubt, because they are the methods of the common law, one of the most creative legal systems the world has seen. And it must be repeated that we have already used and currently do use both of them for the shaping of constitutional rights *not* enumerated; all we need to do is cease to duck our heads in embarrassment about this entirely creditable fact, and let these methods loose, for the work of law-finding that they surely can perform.

We are committed, moreover, to certain root-values: "liberty," "equality," the right to "the pursuit of happiness," and others as well. This commitment is unusually clear in our case; it was undertaken in the organic act that made us an independent nation, and in the words in which we first stated the goals of our political organization, as that structure stands today. Commitment to these values is too vague for use in law, *in part of their range.* But as to some other parts of that range, it is possible to deduce rights usable in constitutional law; I have tendered a vastly important rule of "proportionality" as an example of this, and have suggested one or two others.

In these methods, we have ample means of making out—*for ourselves,* because it has not been done for us positively or negatively, early or late—what it is that the Ninth Amendment is guarding against denial and disparagement. What can and should result is a systematic corpus of the law and equity of human rights, under our Constitution. We will not all agree with every conclusion on which the legal system as a whole settles; this disagreement will exist because the methods we have to use do not produce demonstrable certainty. In other words, we are dealing with *law,* and our systematic corpus of constitutionally guarded human rights will have the characteristics of all law. If we build this corpus, we will do so fallibly; the product will have flaws. If we do not build it, we will have attained certainty—the certainty of unflawed injustice.

I think I ought to repeat that, unless we are to see a massive overruling of cases, some of which are now in their second century, *we are going to be protecting rights not named in the Constitution.* We do that already, under a variety of explanations, the most bizarre of which is doubtless the concept of "*substantive due process.*" That teasingly paradoxical phrase is the competition to a frank acceptance of the invitation to use our sanctioned legal methods in an unembarrassed and never-to-be-finished building of a well-joined edifice of binding human-rights law.

I have a final thought about the general shape of that edifice of law—and in that thought may be contained not only a vision of a goal but also a further methodologic canon. There doubtless never was, historically, a "social contract." But our legal system very often *implies* or *postulates* "contracts" that we know were never actually entered into, for the purpose of doing justice and equity. These have been named "quasi-contracts"; we have constructed them when it seemed that a person ought equitably to be treated *as though* bound by a "contract," and the terms of these quasi-contracts have been settled by asking, "what, under the circumstances, ought this person be *taken* to have agreed to do, in order that justice be done?" There is no reason why a

Social Quasi-contract might not be given shape, binding the government (and, in proper cases, one's fellow-citizens) to forbearances and actions. We would have to ask, for example, "what are the terms of the quasi-contract that this political society ought to be *treated* as having entered into, when it commands and forces its members to abstain from violence and fraud in their attempt to feed their children and themselves? Or when it drafts them into its armies?"

The resultant scope and tenor of this Social Quasi-contract would, obviously, overlap largely with the protections and affirmative assurances resulting from the methods already discussed. This reinforcement of one line of reasoning by another equally valid is a characteristic of all well-developed and complex systems; mathematics is the paradigm. And we might remember, also, that the line is not always easily drawn, in private law, between the contract implied-in-law—the true quasi-contract—and the contract implied-in-fact. A nation that declares itself founded, partly, to "promote the general welfare," may be thought to have undertaken, by implication-in-fact, that welfare is to be generally diffused. The Social Quasi-contract may be thought to contain much the same term, for reasons already hinted at. And so on. The "citizenship" concept and promise, textually locked into the Fourteenth Amendment, may be a bridge between these two modes. We should make the most of these resonances; where they are audible, they powerfully confirm the rightness of any conclusion.

This invocation of the private-law concept of quasi-contract, as a conceivable part of the constitutional law of human rights, should strongly remind us that our Constitution is a part of the "Law of the Land"—by express command of Article VI, and by an implication that would have been a necessary one even if Article VI had not contained the phrase. It is an integral part of the legal system within which it has been placed. There is no reason why it ought not use the methods of that system—of its "Law and Equity," as Article III irresistibly implies. In one aspect, the unitary thesis of this article has been that the construction of a general system of human-rights constitutional law not only demands but deserves the use of the full methodologic set of tools, small and large, that are contained within and accepted by the legal system with which the Constitution is united and blended.

At least no one can say there is no worthy work for law or lawyers in the decades to come, if we have the courage to take that work upon us—the courage to enter and cultivate the field that the Ninth Amendment fences and guards.

GLASSBORO STATE COLLEGE